D1739074

I'm Sorry
about the Clock

I'm Sorry about the Clock

Chronology, Composition, and Narrative Technique in *The Great Gatsby*

Thomas A. Pendleton

SUP

Selinsgrove: Susquehanna University Press
London and Toronto: Associated University Presses

Associated University Presses
440 Forsgate Drive
Cranbury, NJ 08512

Associated University Presses
25 Sicilian Avenue
London WC1A 2QH, England

Associated University Presses
P.O. Box 338, Port Credit
Mississauga, Ontario
Canada L5G 4L8

The paper used in this publication meets the requirements of the American National Standard for Permanence of Paper for Printed Library Materials Z39.48-1984.

Library of Congress Cataloging-in-Publication Data

Pendleton, Thomas A.
    I'm sorry about the clock : chronology, composition, and narrative technique in The great Gatsby / Thomas A. Pendleton.
        p.cm.
    Includes bibliographical references and index.
    ISBN 0-945636-38-5 (alk. paper)
    1. Fitzgerald, F. Scott (Francis Scott), 1896–1940.   Great Gatsby.
2. Fitzgerald, F. Scott (Francis Scott), 1896–1940—Technique.
3. Chronology in literature.   4. Narration (Rhetoric)   I. Title.
PS3511.I9G868   1993
813'.52—dc20   91-51135
                                                                                CIP

Contents

Acknowledgments

Among those whose help I must acknowledge are my colleagues and friends in the English Department of Iona College: Jim Brophy, George Little, John Mahon, Bill McGlone, Michael Palma, Barbara Solomon, Ric Winslow, and others whom I have forgotten; they have put up with my nattering on about this far beyond the call of duty. The secretarial services of the college, especially Mary Bruno and Nancy Girardi, prepared more versions of this study than any of us like to recall; and the staff of the Ryan Library, especially the late John Neuherz, were more than helpful in obtaining materials for me.

I would also like to express my appreciation to a scholar whom I have not met and who I am sure would disagree with many of my conclusions in this study. It would have been quite literally impossible for me to do this examination without the textual studies of Professor Matthew J. Bruccoli of the University of South Carolina. I hope that does not sound too much like Luther being grateful to Pope Julius, but if it is the curse of the great scholar that his work supports that with which he disagrees, it is also his accolade.

I must also acknowledge a permanent debt to my mentor, the late Professor Erwin W. Geissman of Fordham University. He was an inspiring scholar and the best teacher I have ever encountered. Most of what I know about literature I learned from him, and this would have been a better book had he lived long enough to read it in draft.

My wife, Carol, was as always loving and supportive.

I'm Sorry
about the Clock

1

Introduction

The artistry of *The Great Gatsby* has elicited a number of notably unrestrained commendations: James E. Miller, Jr., spoke of its "absolute certainty of control."[1] William A. Fahey called it "by almost any standard a nearly perfect book" and claimed that "even the minor details of the novel are handled with absolute success";[2] Maxwell Geismar rated it "the most perfect example of a planned novel in our modern tradition";[3] and Edmund Wilson asserted that "every word, every cadence, every detail [performs] a definite function in producing an intense effect."[4] More recent critics are equally laudatory: for Brian Way it is a work of "faultless artistry";[5] for Harold Bloom "a book in which nothing is aesthetically wasted";[6] for Matthew J. Bruccoli "a triumph of craftmanship";[7] and for Gore Vidal "a small but perfect operation."[8] George Garrett summarizes neatly: *Gatsby* "is by acclamation taken as nearly perfect in all details."[9] For the *ne plus ultra*, however, Charles Thomas Samuels decided that "*The Great Gatsby* is a novel for which a writer might give his life."[10]

Such hyperbole is surely a very small critical sin; for the quality these writers exaggerate is in fact validly present and genuinely admirable in *Gatsby*. Its incidents are vivid and well chosen; its language elegant and evocative; its image patterns intricate and resonant. As a result, it impresses the reader as an exceptionally finished and polished work. The adjective "lapidary" suggests itself inevitably, and indeed, in his dedicatory verses to *The Crack-Up*, Edmund Wilson imaged *Gatsby* as an emerald "cut consummately."[11] Thus, it is quite surprising to discover that the novel contains a large number of errors in the incidentals of its narrative. Fitzgerald gave Astoria an elevated railroad that belongs in Long Island City, Penn Station a lower level, and young Jimmy Gatz a copy of *Hopalong Cassidy* four years before its publication. And only the intervention of Ring Lardner prevented him from imposing an ebb tide on Lake Superior.[12]

Comparable, but far more surprising and far more significant
to the achievement of this seemingly flawless book, are the con-
tinual incoherences in Fitzgerald's management of the chronology. Difficulties, improbabilities, and flat contradictions beset
both the "present" of *Gatsby*—the summer of 1922—and the past
that vitiates it—especially the past five years of Gatsby's devotion
to Daisy.[13]

These incoherences are the data of this study, which proposes
to utilize them in three ways. First, it will simply demonstrate
that they do in fact occur in the narration; second, it will present
what evidence there is of how and why they occurred; and finally, it will evaluate their significance to the achievement of the
novel.

Mere factual demonstration of these chronological incoherences is in order because, in spite of the abundant and extremely
detailed criticism *Gatsby* has generated, amazingly, almost none
of them seems to have been noted previously. Even those critics
who have written most extensively and most perceptively of the
novel appear unaware of the inconsistencies of its time schemes.

Miller, for example, has produced the classic explication of the
narrative technique of *Gatsby*, and he is especially good on the
purposeful disordering of the story of Gatsby's past. But, in that
very discussion, Miller speaks of "the straight chronological account of the summer of 1922,"[14] clearly not recognizing one of
the novel's most obvious chronological incoherences—that (as
will be shown) Myrtle's party in chapter 2 is later than Gatsby's
in chapter 3. Kenneth Eble is even more subtle and perceptive
about the narration of the novel's present time. Yet immediately
after stating that the summer's chronology "does not move
straightforwardly along,"[15] Eble, too, discusses the opening phase
of *Gatsby* as if Myrtle's party were in proper sequence. Robert E.
Long, who has written a valuable book-length study of *Gatsby*,
also is obviously unaware of this fact, since he adduces as one
of the book's myriad patterns "a continuance in time"[16] based
on the varying times of day presented in the first three chapters.
Long's book contains an impressive amount of material on
Gatsby's literary connections, its relation to Fitzgerald's earlier
fiction, its stages of revision, its thematic structure, and so on.
But the only evidences I discern of recognition that there is anything untoward in the novel's handling of time are the mistaken
references to "the past of two autumns in Louisville" and to
"Gatsby's revisiting Louisville an autumn later,"[17] which may
derive from the realization that something is wrong (as indeed

it is) with Gatsby's poignant departure from "the spring fields" (p. 102).

Overwhelmingly, the critical consensus on the novel has asserted that its greatness as fiction resides in its totally successful disposition of particularities to attain artistic ends. The integration of its narrative details has been claimed to be nearly flawless, certainly exquisitely well performed. As I have indicated, the novel's chronology has previously been almost completely unexamined, but, within this critical context, surely an intricate and successful patterning of temporal details would seem a necessary corollary, and has in fact been categorically asserted by Long: "Fitzgerald's handling of time may deservedly be called masterful; time broken up and scattered through the work has been used in *every* instance with maximum aesthetic effect. . . ."[18]

It is most surprising that there is no recognition in the work of Matthew J. Bruccoli of how frequently chronological incoherence occurs in *Gatsby*. Bruccoli's admirable *Apparatus* for a definitive edition will be cited here repeatedly for matters of factual background, and its explanatory notes do concern themselves with chronological errors. However, only two of the literally dozens that occur are noted—the contradiction about the time of Nick's narration and the error in Pammy's age.[19] Yet Bruccoli is much aware of comparable problems in Fitzgerald's next novel, *Tender Is the Night*. In his recent biography of the author, he claims that the major reason for the reviewers' dissatisfaction with the portrayal of Dick Diver's collapse was "that the time scheme of *Tender* is unclear or even contradictory, and this problem bears on the structure," and he even apportions some of the blame to Maxwell Perkins: "The fault was the author's, but meticulous editing would have called the problem to his attention."[20] Exactly the same judgments may be made about *Gatsby*, but, to the best of my knowledge, neither Bruccoli nor anyone else has made them.

It should be unnecessary to state that I do not write in disparagement of these investigators of *Gatsby*. Quite to the contrary, my point is that the novel's chronological inconsistences have passed unnoticed by even the best of its critics. Whether or not one agrees with the significances I will attach to those inconsistencies, it must, I think, be allowed that the fact of their existence should be noted.

The second object of this study is to examine the *why* of these inconsistencies, and it is demonstrable that a great many of them were caused, or at least influenced, by Fitzgerald's progressive revisions of the novel. In detail, his process of composition and revision was extremely complicated, but it can, without serious misrepresentation, be thought of as having occurred in three stages, corresponding to the kinds of textual material that have survived.

The earliest state of *Gatsby*'s development is represented by the manuscript—a holograph draft of 264 pages. In time, most of this material was written after April 1924, once Fitzgerald had managed to clear off his debts with a spate of short stories and was able to devote full time to *Gatsby*. Individual elements, however, may well date back at least to June of 1923, when he began on the novel, only to put it aside to work on his ill-fated play, *The Vegetable*. Virtually all of the manuscript appears to predate September 1924, when, according to his ledger, he undertook a thorough revision that produced the next level of composition.[21]

The manuscript can be read through as a reasonably coherent narrative, but, in fact, it does not represent a single state of composition. Rather, it is a collection of pages written at various times over a period of five months or more; some of them recopied from earlier, nonextant drafts; almost all containing pencilled cancellations and changes inserted both during composition and later; many embodying contradictions of materials on other pages.[22] It is very much a working draft, conflating many layers of composition and leaving many of the novel's final decisions yet to be made.

Between about September and the beginning of November 1924, Fitzgerald brought the novel to a final typescript copy, which he sent to his editor, Maxwell Perkins, and which elicited Perkins's perceptive and justly famous response of 20 November 1924. The typescript is apparently lost, but, except for accidentals of house-styling and the like, it must have corresponded to the surviving set of unrevised galleys.[23] Unlike the manuscript version, the typescript version does represent a single stage of composition that the novel had reached. The nine chapters are now in the order in which they appear in the published novel, with Myrtle's party as the second chapter and the passage on Nick's wanderings in New York and his house party at Warwick with Jordan as the conclusion of chapter 3. In effect, the typescript version gives us the first five chapters and the last in something close to their final form; the sixth, seventh, and eighth chapters were yet to undergo quite substantial revision.

The last stage of Fitzgerald's composition is demonstrated by the revised galleys in the collection of the Firestone Library at Princeton.[24] The revisions embodied here belong to January and February of 1925; on about 18 February, he returned the last of the revised galleys "after six weeks of uninterrupted work."[25] Aside from a few spot changes and insertions that Fitzgerald sent during the last seven weeks before publication,[26] the revised galleys became the copy for the first edition. There are a multitude of changes from the typescript version. As has been discussed fairly often, Fitzgerald substantially rewrote the confrontation of Tom and Gatsby at the Plaza—a scene with which he was never fully satisfied. He also moved the account of Gatsby's years with Dan Cody from chapter 8 to the beginning of chapter 6, and the paragraphs on Gatsby's incarnating his aspirations in Daisy from chapter 7 to the end of chapter 6. The resultant effect of gradual revelation of the truth was a masterly stroke, and has been much and properly praised.

Over the past twenty years or so, there have been a number of quite valuable studies of the draft materials for *Gatsby*, to which this work is, of course, indebted.[27] Like most criticism of the novel, these studies have been highly adulatory, focusing especially on Fitzgerald's relocation of events and his verbal polishing as evidence of a masterful craftsmanship. Their total effect, I think, may be communicated by A. Scott Berg's summary judgment in his biography of Maxwell Perkins: "F. Scott Fitzgerald is generally regarded as having been his own best editor, as having had the patience and objectivity to read his words over and over again, eliminating flaws and perfecting his prose."[28]

Again, this study proposes an exception to the critical consensus; for although Fitzgerald's revisions achieved much that is praiseworthy, they also introduced a great many of the temporal incoherences. Further, it is demonstrable that a considerable number of these incoherences were the results of Fitzgerald's much praised repositioning of materials. We know from the manuscript the order in which the incidents of the first five chapters were composed and how they were originally intended to be arranged. From the typescript version on, however, the rearrangement of these incidents almost invariably causes incoherence because the original tonalities or the originally intended interrelationships among them are inappropriate to the new locations. Finally, while the general success of Fitzgerald's revision of even minute verbal details must also be allowed, a comparably narrow focus sometimes led him to revise a coherent temporal detail into incoherence for the sake of some local, nontemporal effect.

Investigation of the management of chronology in *Gatsby* can demonstrate quite factually both that the novel's patterning of narrative detail is something less than flawless and also that many of the flaws derive from something less than impeccable revision. The last of this study's three aims, however—to evaluate the significance of the chronological inconsistencies—is a judgmental matter that admits of no such surety. This kind of judgment is more appropriately presented as the more or less grievous instances of temporal incoherence are investigated, and then brought to a final evaluation after the total evidences have been considered. For the moment, however, two relatively theoretical positions may be worthwhile asserting.

First, it is in the nature of fiction itself that narrative discrepancies such as chronological incoherence always "matter" to some degree. Although the writer of fiction ultimately does not claim that his story is true, by definition he speaks of it as if it were. He presents, therefore, an illusion that has meaning only by its referential relationship to the nonfictional, experiential, "true" world of his readers. It is all but an unavoidable metaphor to speak of "the world" of a novel because the fictive illusion is formally presented as if it were experiential reality; and thus we judge the meaning, value, and artistry of the novel by its reflection or correspondence or contradiction or criticism or exaltation or denigration of the world outside fiction in which we live.

We know the novel is an illusion, just as we know the magician doesn't really saw the lady in half, but we suppress our knowledge. If we were to see the lady's feet tucked up above the saw blade, we could not respond to the illusion as if it were reality, because we would be conscious that it is nothing but an illusion, or (better, perhaps) nothing but a clumsily handled bit of experiential reality trying to sustain itself as an illusion.

Errors in the fictive illusion similarly erode the suspension of disbelief necessary to experience the illusion as if it were real by forcing us to be conscious of the manipulator of the illusion. A single error is seldom, perhaps never, totally destructive; it may well be negligible. Any number of readers of *Gatsby*, I expect, have noticed the contradictions about Pammy's age, have suppressed that consciousness, and have lost very little in their experience of the novel. But errors that are more grievous, or that are tactically more important to the narrative, or that simply are numerous weigh more heavily against the maintenance of the fictive illusion; and all three cases apply in *Gatsby*.

Secondly, the temporal incoherences are of somewhat more gravity because of the narrative method Fitzgerald has chosen for his novel. *The Great Gatsby* is, to use Fitzgerald's own term, a "novel of selected incidents."[29] As is often noted, it fully renders only a few events, usually one or two dramatized scenes per chapter. Many other events are mentioned only in passing, such as Jordan's leaving the borrowed car in the rain; others are included within narrative generalities, such as Nick's twilight wanderings in New York City; still others are omitted from mention totally, or all but totally, yet are understood to have occurred, such as the further parties Nick attends at Gatsby's or the further assignations Tom has with Myrtle.

Ordinarily, the interrelation of the dramatized scenes and the lesser events operates quite well to create a reliable fictional world. To illustrate negatively, we can say with certainty that Nick does not invite Wolfsheim to dine at the Yale Club, Tom does not seduce Jordan, and Gatsby does not steal Myrtle's dog— not because the narrative says these things do not occur, but because their occurrence would be so outrageously inconsistent with what the narrative does say.

In his own comments on the composition of *Gatsby*, Fitzgerald often revealed his concern with just this kind of consistency. In December 1924, in reply to Perkins' remarkable analysis of the strengths and weaknesses of the draft he had read, Fitzgerald confessed that Gatsby was vague because *"I myself didn't know what Gatsby looked like or was engaged in,"* and then boasted with the elation of discovery, "I know Gatsby better than I know my own child."[30] On 9 August 1925, depressed by the sales of the book, he admitted to John Peale Bishop, "Also you are right about Gatsby being blurred and patchy. I never at any one time saw him clear myself."[31] And about the same time, he chortled to Edmund Wilson, like a schoolboy who had passed a test without studying:

> The worst fault in it, I think it is a BIG FAULT: I gave no account (and had no feeling about or knowledge of) the emotional relations between Gatsby and Daisy from the time of their reunion to the catastrophe. However the lack is so astutely concealed by the retrospect of Gatsby's past and by blankets of excellent prose that no one has noticed it—though everyone has felt the lack and called it by another name.[32]

The one common element in this various (and rather touching) testimony is an immediate willingness to account for what succeeds or fails in *Gatsby* in terms of an imaginative knowledge of the story and the characters, which must be complete and consistent in the author's mind, even though it is not completely adumbrated in the narrative. Bruccoli cogently relates this attitude to "Hemingway's iceberg theory of composition that an author can omit anything he knows from a story without damaging it. Using the iceberg analogy, Hemingway argued that the force of a story results from its hidden part."[33] It would seem that such a technique requires critical inquiry into the implicit coherence of the portions of the story above the surface with those below, and perhaps requires even more stringently that the limited number of elements actually posited cohere totally with one another.

Obviously, one dimension of this coherence is the temporal, because the characters live and the events interrelate in time. Myrtle screams at Wilson just before she runs out to her death, Nick returns to Gatsby watching over nothing after he has seen Tom and Daisy conspiring, Tom and Sloane leave Gatsby's while he is getting ready to accompany them, Nick hears of Gatsby and of Tom's infidelity for the first time during the dinner, Gatsby does not use his pool until the day of his death. In every case—and the list could be extended indefinitely—the temporal indication is constitutive to the quality and meaning of the scene. As will be frequently mentioned, the five years of Gatsby's devotion is an index of its intensity, and the three months of the summer in Nick's retrospect is a startlingly brief time for the critical changes it contains. Even recognizing that Tom torments Wilson about selling the car from sometime before July until the very end of August provides a convincing illustration of how practiced a sadist and how confirmed a victim they are respectively. It is just this aspect of illuminating relationships and qualities that the chronological discrepancies in *Gatsby* frequently at least weaken and sometimes destroy.

The amount and complexity of the material to be considered is such that this study will deal with the events of the novel's present and its past separately. Since the narrative order of the nine chapters, with one exception, coincides with the course of the summer of 1922, the chapters will be investigated in sequence to locate their major events within the summer and to indicate what chronological difficulties they present. Various

lesser or wider matters of chronology will be dealt with in reference to the chapter that seems most appropriate.

The references to the past are scattered nonsequentially
throughout all nine of the chapters. So here the plan is to deal
first with the relatively little information provided about the major characters—most noteworthy, of course, about Gatsby—prior
to the romance in Louisville; then, since it is the most detailed
and comprehensive presentation of the years 1917 to 1921, Jordan Baker's account in chapter 4 will be utilized as a matrix to
examine the five years of Gatsby's devotion.

Two last preliminaries. Formally, it is the "real" calendar for
1922 and no other that Fitzgerald posited for his fiction, but that
calendar will be adverted to here only two or three times and
then largely for the purpose of demonstrating its inconsequence.
Fitzgerald clearly did not use it in planning Gatsby, and nowhere
in the text does he indicate a date so specifically as to demand
one and only one placement on the 1922 calendar. Strictly
speaking, there is, I suppose, some element of chronological incoherence and imperfect verisimilitude implied by these facts,
but this study will concern itself with incoherence within the
temporal structures Fitzgerald did indicate in the narrative of
Gatsby. From this point of view the 1922 calendar is simply an
irrelevance.

Finally, I am of course aware that to approach so admired a
book as Gatsby in the manner I propose runs the risk of ap-
pearing ferociously literal-minded and thus, perhaps, insensitive
to its remarkable achievements. This is not the place to attempt
a precise calculation of the significance of the chronological incoherences to be presented, but an outward limit of sanity might
be suggested: I, of course, do not suppose that they are so significant as to negate the book's quite substantial virtues and to eradi-
cate it from further consideration.

As to literal-mindedness, it can only be answered that this
study proposes to investigate time in Gatsby not as a dimension
or an illusion or a limitation on romantic idealism—all of which
are significant—but time as chronology—measured time, calendar time, clock time. And chronology is a literal matter.

As to sensitivity or insensitivity, I suppose one must take his
chances.

2

The Chronology of the Present

Chapter 1 (The Dinner at the Buchanans')

The first chapter, in part because it is the first chapter, presents no chronological problems. On the contrary, it deals with two temporal matters quite firmly: it dates the major narrative event reliably, and it strongly suggests the summer of 1922 as a unified time frame.

The major narrative event is, of course, the dinner party that Nick attends at Tom and Daisy's house, and it is located in time by Daisy's "In two weeks it'll be the longest day of the year" (p. 8). The conversational form does not invite to literalism, and one would hardly expect precision from Daisy. Still, the comment is so patently Fitzgerald's means of placing the event in time that one can conclude that Daisy is basically accurate and that the dinner occurs—give or take a bit—fourteen days before the summer solstice; thus, about 7 June.

Corroboration seems hardly necessary, but some is available. On the evening of Myrtle's death—which occurs unmistakably at the very end of August—Nick recalls the Buchanans' dinner as "that June night three months before" (p. 97). After Jordan's narrative in chapter 4, he remembers seeing Gatsby on the evening of the dinner, "on that June night" (p. 52). And here in the opening chapter, he states that "the history of the summer really begins" (p. 4) on that night. All these point at least to the dinner's occurring in early June.

The "history of the summer" comment is also the most significant of a number of passages in chapter 1 that imply the integrity of the summer as a time frame. If there is a "history of the summer," presumably there is coterminous with the summer a narrative complete, unified, and chronologically coherent. The implication is all the stronger in view of the chapter's opening retrospective paragraphs, in which Nick speaks from the vantage point of having completed an experience that left him wanting "no more riotous excursions with privileged glimpses into the human heart" (p. 1). Clearly, Gatsby was central to the experience, for "Gatsby turned out all right at the end" (p. 2). Implicitly, the experience belongs to the summer, for it was completed by the time that Nick "came back from the East last autumn" (p. 1).

Equally significant is Nick's recollection of his sense of the beginning of summer as a time of opportunity and expectation, a human season: "And so with the sunshine and the great bursts of leaves growing on the trees, just as things grow in fast movies, I had that familiar conviction that life was beginning over again with the summer" (p. 3). Since there is an obvious invitation to the reader to anticipate the fulfillment or frustration of these summer hopes, it seems a fair inference that Fitzgerald has suggested that the progress of the summer will be concordant with the progress of the human expectations, and thus the coherence of the human experience should imply a comparable temporal coherence.

Among minor matters, the chapter provides an anticipatory reference to Gatsby by Jordan during the dinner and, of course, a brief, mysterious glimpse of Gatsby, yearning through the darkness toward the green light on Daisy's dock. Jordan's mention of Gatsby, her playing in a golf tournament on the day after the Buchanans' dinner, and the scandal of her cheating that eludes Nick's recollection—all will serve as points of reference for later events.

It is also worth noting Fitzgerald's usage of the word *summer*. Although the season does not officially begin until June 21— Daisy's "longest day in the year"—Fitzgerald, like most of us most of the time, thinks of summer as the months of June, July, and August. Thus, "life was beginning over again with the summer," presumably at the beginning of June; "the history of the summer begins" with the Buchanans' dinner about a week into June; and when Nick drives home, "already it was deep summer" (p. 14). The usage of *summer* is quite consistent; so too will be references to the other seasons.

The earlier drafts of chapter 1 create no difficulty; rather they make it clear that, from the earliest stages of composition, Fitzgerald had decided what to begin with and how to locate it. The manuscript contains Daisy's references to the longest day of the year and to the golf tournament, Jordan's mention of Gatsby, and his brief appearance. Fitzgerald canceled "a warm June evening" and a "June evening" (MS, p. 10), before settling for "a warm windy evening" (MS, p. 10), as in the final text, for the dinner.

From the beginning, he had chosen his tactics for dating the action and providing for reference to events to come.

Finally, the first chapter contains a literal misstatement of fact, which is of less significance as a misstatement than as a means of engaging a significant element in the narrative method of *Gatsby* and two incoherences in its utilization. Nick says, "why they [Tom and Daisy] came East I don't know" (p. 4), which, strictly speaking, is untrue. The narration occurs in 1923 or 1924; Gatsby is already dead and his dream shattered; and Nick has already heard Daisy say in the Plaza scene, "Do you know why we left Chicago? I'm surprised they didn't treat you to the story of that little spree" (p. 88). At the time of the narration—what for the moment may be called the formal present—Nick knows that the Buchanans came east because of Tom's scandalous infidelity. But in terms of the action of the summer of 1922—what may be called the effective present—he has yet to learn this. As is almost always the case in *Gatsby*, the summer of 1922 is being treated as present experience, and the reader is being limited to what Nick knows at the relevant time during that summer.

This literal contradiction is not of much weight; one must force the present tense rather hard to demonstrate it. It is not the lack of control of this minutia of chronology that is so much worth noting as that it results from Fitzgerald's having distanced his narrator in time from the story he has to tell. In general, the tactic is successful enough, for the location in time is nicely coherent with the tonalities of poignancy, regret, disapproval, and finality that belong to the older Nick who tells the story, not to Nick the apprentice stockbroker who participated in it. And we are reminded of the older Nick—by the faded timetable, for instance—just about often enough, I think, to retain those tonalities.

In most fiction, even in most first-person retrospectives, it is virtually a convention of the form to allow the fact of the story's being told to pass without scrutiny. We do not know, for example, the immediate motive or occasion for Pip's recounting the story of his great expectations, but our ignorance arouses no dissatisfaction. On the other hand, when the novel specifically engages these problems of motive and occasion, we reasonably expect that the engagement be a purposeful element in the overall fictional strategy. To advert to a work often compared to *Gatsby*, Conrad's *Heart of Darkness* engages these problems by supplying the frame of Marlow's addressing his friends on the yacht, and the fact of the presentation of the tale to this circle of moral connoisseurs clearly bears on the depth and universal applicability both Marlow and Conrad insist the tale possesses.

In effect, the narrative of *Gatsby* operates rather more like *Great Expectations* than *Heart of Darkness* in this regard. We accept that the older Nick, like the older Pip, is distanced in time and feeling, and that his more youthful excitements and hopes are now lightly coated with the dust of his later and sadder perception. But there is nothing in terms of exactly why, to whom, or under what circumstances Nick tells his tale that sharpens or illuminates our insight into the quality of his evaluation of that tale. This is to say, in effect, that Fitzgerald has availed himself of the convention of leaving the provenance of the narration itself unexamined. In contradiction of this effect, however, he has formally posited as part of the fictional structure an engagement of these concerns: Nick proposes himself not just as the teller of a story, but as the writer of a book.

This would seem necessarily a significant element of the novel's narrative method, for, if the narrator is actually composing his narration in book form, he is consciously structuring, interpreting, and evaluating, and thus his disassociation from the events he relates is formalized and emphasized considerably beyond what unexamined narration implies. Such a difference is in fact a constitutive element in any number of novels. To cite two ready examples, in Vonnegut's *Mother Night*, the essentially sane but unprincipled Howard J. Campbell composes, while in an Israeli prison, a sort of *apologia* for his war crimes and, in doing so, persuades himself that the logical culmination of his experience is to commit suicide; and in a more bizarrely ironic context, the essentially mad Charles Kinbote in Nabakov's *Pale Fire* roams off into his own delusions and fantasies in the course of ostensibly preparing a posthumous edition of the last work of the poet John Shade.

Nothing remotely like this, however, occurs with Nick's authorship in *Gatsby*. If we think of *Great Expectations*, *Heart of Darkness*, and either *Mother Night* or *Pale Fire* as establishing an increasing scale of formalized distancing of the narrator from his narration, it appears that Fitzgerald has posited something close to Vonnegut or Nabakov, but has achieved something close to Dickens. For the references to Nick as author are simply neither frequent enough, nor emphatic enough to make any practical difference to the narration. There are in fact only three such references: here in the first chapter Nick refers to Gatsby as "the man who gives his name to this book" (p. 1); at the transition to the closing section of chapter 3, Nick speaks of "reading over what I have written so far" (p. 37); and after telling the Dan Cody story in chapter 6, he says that Gatsby "told me all this very much later, but I've put it down here" (p. 67).

Samuels argues that "Nick is writing a book. He is recording Gatsby's experience; in the act of recording Gatsby's experience he discovers himself" and that "In writing about Gatsby, Nick alters his attitude toward his subject and ultimately toward his own life."[1] But palpably this is not what happens, for the "boats against the current" coda (which Samuels accepts as the final discovery) is delivered, Nick tells us, "as I sat there brooding" (p. 121) in the fall of 1922, not after writing the book, some two years later.

Garrett deals with this matter far more subtly, emphasizing the sense of Nick's narrative being in the process of composition. He notes the use of devices such as present-tense aphoristic judgments, such as "There is no confusion like the confusion of a simple mind" (p. 149), and acts of present memory, such as "I think he'd tanked up a good deal at luncheon" (p. 28), and finds them used "to focus our attention on aftermath, to emphasize reaction more than action" (which I think verges on overstatement), and "to set in some sense of tension, if not conflict, often within the same sentence, the qualities of the spoken versus the written."[2] Nick's narration presents the written American vernacular, in its "range, suppleness, and eloquence,"[3] and is set in contrast not just to the dialogue within the dramatic scenes, but even (as with "I think he'd tanked up") to elements in the narration itself. As a result, Garrett finds, Nick as narrator develops a linguistic virtuosity that will then be exploited for and will justify the book's narrative virtuosity, most notably when Nick's narration performs the tasks of authorial omniscience.

Although I prefer to defer discussion of this last point, Garrett's approach (as one would expect from so talented as novelist) is perceptive and to a large degree convincing. Obviously, he has used his awareness of the device of Nick as author to develop an illuminating perspective on the book's style. But the implication that the written, as opposed to spoken, orientation of Nick's narration constantly reminds the reader that Nick is engaged in writing simply cannot be allowed. Almost any but the most relentlessly colloquial narrator will deal to some degree in the written vernacular; both Pip's and Marlow's narrations are oriented far more to the written than the spoken language, and even within *Gatsby*, Jordan's narration in chapter 3—"in a credible and appropriate vernacular,"[4] as Garrett says—utilizes the written as well as the spoken.

For Nick as author to operate as a constitutive element in the novel, a great deal more adversion to the fact would be necessary. But Garrett finds no more such references than I do.

In fact, the total absence of any reminder of Nick's authorship as the narrative is concluded in the ninth chapter argues against making anything of the device. Since the allusion to the title in chapter 1 and Nick's "reading over" in chapter 3 frame what is universally recognized as the novel's first movement, and since no hint of Nick the author beyond the rather oblique "I've put it down here" appears in the remaining two-thirds of *Gatsby*, I suspect that Fitzgerald, as he wrote on into the novel, simply forgot from time to time that he had posited such a device.

The allusion to the book's title, incidentally, has the quite odd implication that Nick has written not just a book, but this book— *The Great Gatsby*. This gives rise to the even odder question of identifying the F. Scott Fitzgerald who has managed to get his name on Nick's title page. Obviously, this kind of concern can be dealt with only at the level of a Baker Street Irregular's mock-solemn explanation of Conan Doyle's access to Watson's notes.

That such meager and purposeless vestiges survive of what logically should have been a salient factor in the narration is hardly to Fitzgerald's credit as a craftsman. In point of fact, however, he was fortunate that he made virtually nothing of the device of Nick as author, because, as a device, it was quite ill chosen. If one were to take the device seriously, he would have to suppose that Nick is planning to publish a scandalous exposé. For if Nick is author, his book itself becomes an artifact of his fictional world, even as Gatsby's car and Wolfsheim's cufflinks are. There is no sense that Nick is compiling a private communication or a secret journal; everything he states seems addressed to a general audience: and, thus, his book would make known to his world any number of shocking and previously secret matters. Nick's book would publicize the scandal of Jordan's cheating, which had only been whispered about; it would document the adulteries of both Buchanans;[5] it would accuse Daisy of vehicular homicide, Tom as an accessory before the fact of Gatsby's murder, and Nick himself as accessory after the fact of both crimes for having concealed them for a year or more.[6]

But no such intentions are discernible in the text of the novel. To the contrary, the text insists that "the one unutterable fact" (p. 120) for Nick would be to tell Tom who had driven the death car. He would, of course, be uttering this unutterable fact if he were writing a book; and, although Nick says that he "couldn't forgive . . . or like" Tom, his dismissing Tom from mature moral responsibility—"I felt suddenly as though I were talking to a child" (p. 120)—precludes shattering him with the knowledge of Daisy's guilt.

Fitzgerald gives little evidence of having thought through the fictional implications of making Nick an author. But he was saved from those implications by his own inattention to the device. The outcome was fortuitous, but this is scarcely a masterful playing of the game of art.[7]

There is also a second, and simpler, incoherence connected to Nick's narrating his story, and it has already been mentioned. The novel contradicts itself about when the narration occurs. Here in the opening chapter, the "now" of Nick's narrating is established by his "when I came back from the East last autumn" (p. 1), which requires that he tell the story before the winter of 1923. On the other hand, the last chapter opens with Nick, "after two years" (p. 109), remembering the day of Gatsby's death, thus placing the "now" of his narration in September 1924 at the earliest. Bruccoli broaches the possibility that Fitzgerald may have intended the disparate statements to indicate the elapsing of a year while Nick writes his book.[8] But, as has been demonstrated, the emphasis on Nick's authorship is too weak to support the suggestion, nor does the novel contain any evidence that Nick's attitude about the totality of his experience changes or develops during his narrating that experience, thus implying an accompanying passage of time. There can hardly be any real doubt that the disagreement between the two statements is simply an error on Fitzgerald's part.

Chapter 2 (Myrtle's Party)

With chapter 2, severe problems of chronology develop, although ironically the major narrative event is located about as firmly as any event in the novel. We are twice told that the party at Myrtle's Washington Heights apartment occurs on a Sunday (pp. 16, 18), and further that "it was a few days before the Fourth of July" (p. 17).

According to the calendar for 1922, when the Fourth fell on a Tuesday, the date would seem to be Sunday, 2 July. This is one of the very rare occasions that the narrative of *Gatsby* provides sufficient detail for a calendar dating, but it should be noted that one arrives at the date only by forcing "a few" to mean literally "two," which, by any precise usage, it does not mean. Such precision might seem unnecessary to Nick's conversational narrative, but it would seem essential if adversion to the actual 1922 calendar were in fact part of the design of *Gatsby*. Thus, the imprecision here rather argues against, not for, the relevance of the calendar.

Far more important, however, is the fact that Myrtle's party, "a few days before the Fourth of July," is out of chronological sequence. It occurs in fact about two weeks after Gatsby's first party, which is the major narrative event of the next chapter and which takes place, as will be demonstrated, in mid-June.

Thus, the placement of the event is in violation of one of the most basic disciplines of the narrative: that the reader will know only what Nick knows and only at the time Nick learns it. Such a demand is perhaps innately part of any first-person retrospective. To use an obvious example, it would seem impossible for the reader to share Nick's sense of strangeness and mystery at the first appearance of Gatsby if, at that time, he knew Gatsby's story and understood the symbolism of the single green light.

It is also a discipline that elsewhere in the novel is observed rather punctiliously. Nick tells the story of Gatsby's years with Dan Cody, but notes, "He told me all this very much later, but I've put it down here" (p. 67). Before tracing Wilson on his journey of revenge, he states, "Now I want to go back a little and tell what happened at the garage after we left there the night before" (p. 104). Even with the detail of Myrtle's death, Nick implies that his information was obtained later: "The young Greek, Michaelis, who ran the coffee joint beside the ashheaps was the principal witness at the inquest" (p. 91).[9] All three examples, it will be noted, are Nick's departures from chronological order to narrate what he has heard, not what he has experienced, and even then he calls attention to these departures. In such a context, the chronological misplacing of the narrative core of a chapter, like Myrtle's party, is an exceptional breach of the novel's temporal discipline.

The breach is considerably more exceptional since Fitzgerald has built into the novel a number of invitations to believe that chapter 2 is in proper chronological sequence. The first two chapters are linked not just by Myrtle's phone call in the first chapter and her appearance in the second, but more strongly by the insistence in both on the notoriety and offensiveness of the adultery. During the dinner party, Jordan says, "I thought every-body knew. . . . Tom's got some woman in New York," and com-plains, "She might have the decency not to telephone him at dinner time. Don't you think?" (pp. 10–11). And in the opening paragraphs of chapter 2, Nick reports, "The fact that he had one [a mistress] was insisted upon wherever he was known. His ac-quaintances resented the fact that he turned up in popular res-taurants with her . . ." (p. 15). The adducing of substantially the same behavior in the successive chapters invites belief in their closeness in time.

To move to chapter 3 for the moment, Nick follows his account of Gatsby's first party by reflecting, "Reading over what I have written so far, I see I have given the impression that the events of three nights several weeks apart were all that absorbed me" (p. 37), a crucial passage that will be adverted to again. The placement of this reflection after the account of Gatsby's party clearly implies that Gatsby's party was the third of the "three nights several weeks apart" (an implication which the drafts of this section validate); in fact, it was the second, and thus is irrele-vant to the duration of the "several weeks." In view of the chro-nology of the published text, the passage in question amounts to a remarkable incoherence, and made all the more remarkable for the apparent invocation of narrative authority with Nick's "Reading over what I have written so far."

Finally, and most strongly, the reader is invited to believe that Myrtle's party is in proper chronology by Catherine's mention of Gatsby and Nick's reply:

> ". . . Do you know him?"
> "I live next door to him."
>
> (p. 21)

The situation is all but identical with Jordan's mention of Gatsby and Nick's response in Chapter 1:

> "You must know Gatsby." . . .
> Before I could reply that he was my neighbor dinner was an-nounced. . . .
>
> (p. 8)[10]

Since Nick responds this way in chapter 1, when he tells us "I hadn't met Mr. Gatsby" (p. 8), the same response in the next chapter, when we have not yet learned of Nick's meeting him, naturally leads to the inference that Catherine's question, and hence Myrtle's party, precedes the introduction of Gatsby in chapter 3.

All of the narrative indications, with the exception of the time reference itself, require that Myrtle's party occur before Gatsby's, but the Fourth of July reference insists that it be later. The self-contradiction is patent and constitutes a significant narrative lapse.

The lapse, it seems certain, was caused by the rather complicated process of composition and revision this portion of the narrative underwent. The chapter on Myrtle's party, in spite of its position in the published text, was not the second, but the fourth to be written. In the manuscript, it is preceded by the early versions of the chapters on the Buchanans' dinner, Gatsby's first party, and the lunch with Wolfsheim—that is, book chapters 1, 3, and 4; these are paginated consecutively and designated in the manuscript as chapters I, II, and III respectively.

The Myrtle's party chapter follows, although in fact it seems never to have been intended as the novel's fourth chapter. In the manuscript, it is numbered, like the lunch with Wolfsheim episode, chapter III. (There is no manuscript chapter IV.) It is in large part a reworking of the Wolfsheim chapter, which, in its earliest form, introduced the valley of ashes, the Wilsons, and the eyes of Dr. Eckleburg,[11] and which had Myrtle reappear in Tom's company during lunch at the Forty-Second Street restaurant. Thus, concomitant with the composition of the Myrtle's party chapter, there would seem to have been an intention to place it in narrative order before the lunch with Wolfsheim. And its being numbered in manuscript as chapter III indicates that it was originally intended to follow Gatsby's party, then manuscript chapter II.

The same original intention is put beyond doubt by the fact that in manuscript Myrtle's party is followed by the first version of the transitional passage already cited: "After reading over what I have written so far I can see that I have given a false impression that the events of three nights, several weeks apart, were all that occupied my mind in the early part of the summer" (MS, p. 120). This is followed by Nick's account of his evenings in Manhattan and his summary of the romance with Jordan, including the house party at Warwick and the "careless driver" conversation (MS, pp. 120–23). In the typescript version, and in the final text of the novel, of course, when Myrtle's party was relocated as the second chapter and before Gatsby's party, the "reading over" transition and the associated materials were kept in place to mark the end of the early part of the summer, but now they were immediately preceded by Gatsby's party, not Myrtle's.

The complication is perhaps sufficient to justify a graphic display of the various orderings of the early incidents in *Gatsby*:

A Order of Composition MS Chapter		B Original Intended Order MS Chapter		C Published Order Book Chapter	
1. The Buchanans' Dinner	I	1. The Buchanans' Dinner	I	1. The Buchanans' Dinner	1
2. Gatsby's Party	II	2. Gatsby's Party	II	2. Myrtle's Party	2
3. The Ride to Manhattan	III_1	3. Myrtle's Party	III_2	3. Gatsby's Party	3
4. Lunch with Wolfsheim	III_1	4. The Warwick Section	III_2	4. The Warwick Section	3
5. Jordan's Narrative	III_1	5. The Ride to Manhattan	III_1	5. The Ride to Manhattan	4
6. The Ride in the Victoria	III_1	6. Lunch with Wolfsheim	III_1	6. Lunch with Wolfsheim	4
7. Myrtle's Party	III_2	7. Jordan's Narrative	III_1	7. Jordan's Narrative	4
8. The Warwick Section	III_2	8. The Ride in the Victoria	III_1	8. The Ride in the Victoria	4

This material is relevant to a number of considerations, but, to return to the matter at hand, the salient point here is that the earliest version of Myrtle's party was immediately followed by the reference to "three nights several weeks apart" that opens the Warwick section, making it clear that originally Myrtle's party was intended to be the third of these nights. It also helps to focus on the incoherence in the final text of placing the "three nights" reference after Gatsby's party, which chronologically is the second of the three.

This is the first of a number of occasions in the early chapters of *Gatsby* when Fitzgerald, at some cost, temporally relocated incidents. Often—as here—the relocation results in incidents that are lacking in some form of coherence because they were originally designed to relate to other events in ways different from those that obtain in the final text.

Why Fitzgerald finally chose to place Myrtle's party as the novel's second chapter can in general terms be answered by the critical approbation of the opening movement of *The Great*

Gatsby. Frederick J. Hoffman, for example, calls the first three chapters "as good an opening as there is in modern fiction."[12] Myrtle's party provides the centerpiece of this opening; it introduces the Wilsons, establishes the symbolic values of the valley of ashes and the eyes of Dr Eckleburg, fully displays Tom's brutality, and—after the Buchanans' and before Gatsby's—demonstrates a third stratum of this fictional society: the grotesque vulgarity of the lower middle class.

Implicitly, Nick's experience in this chapter would also seem of weight in securing the reader's approval of his decision to aid in reuniting Gatsby and Daisy. This is a matter that Fitzgerald had presented quite differently in the manuscript, in which there are frequent indications that Nick is aware that he is abetting an adultery. But all such moralistic concern has been revised out of the published text and, with it, has gone almost all information about why Nick aids the lovers. He characterizes himself as "confused and a little disgusted" (p. 14) after the dinner party, he allows Jordan's "and Daisy ought to have something in her life" (p. 53) to pass without objection, and that is all. His motivation is largely unspecified, but it seems to lie in the direction of sympathy for Daisy's ill treatment, and that implicit justification would, one must suppose, have been much the weaker without the display of Tom's coarseness and cruelty at Myrtle's party.

· The growing acquaintance with the society of the novel and the growing distaste for Tom are, I think, exactly what the reader experiences with Myrtle's party; and, of course, this is also what Nick experiences. But growth exists in time, and the reader's experience is that he is being presented with a sequential progression of events. Surely, no reader has the sense of moving forward in time with Myrtle's party and then backward in time with Gatsby's; no reader presumes that Nick has already met Gatsby, although the time reference insists he has. But if the reader's experience is one of sequential progression and if it is so necessarily keyed to Nick's experience, then Nick's experience too must be one of sequential progression. The implication of the narrative method is unavoidable, yet it is exactly this implication that the time reference disallows.

That the party could have been, even provisionally in Fitzgerald's imagination, either the second or the third chapter of the novel points to a quality that has been relatively little remarked: Myrtle's party is much the most self-contained episode in *Gatsby.*[13] It has much the weakest connection with the novel's plot line, being devoted almost totally to background, thematic materials, and character development. It is the only chapter that makes no significant reference to the past, Myrtle's first meeting with Tom and Catherine's misadventures in Monte Carlo "last year" (p. 22) being inconsequential in these terms. It is also the only chapter—not even excluding the last—in which Gatsby does not appear. Very probably because of this fact, Catherine's anticipatory reference to Gatsby was added in the typescript version. Had there been no reference to Gatsby whatever, the chapter's delay of his appearance might well have seemed not part of the building of expectation, but merely dilatory.

That the chapter is at least potentially digressive can be demonstrated by noting how much more expansive and leisurely its technique is than that of the balance of the novel. The pace and detail, for example, with which the McKees and Catherine are presented is quite different from the introduction of Owl Eyes or even of Wolfsheim. Myrtle's party, brilliant as in many ways it is, might well seem more suitable for a longer and more discursive novel than *Gatsby*. The episode's position as the second chapter much diminishes its potential digressiveness since there is as yet not much narrative impetus from which to digress, and, in a similar way, the early placement of the episode much disguises its chronological incoherence since there is not as yet much narrative sequence to violate. Had Fitzgerald held to his original intention to place Myrtle's party after Gatsby's appearance, it seems safe to assume that its self-containment would have caused a most ineffective intrusion.

But even granting that Myrtle's party all but necessarily had to become the second chapter, there still remains the question of why Fitzgerald added in the typescript the Fourth of July reference which puts the episode out of proper temporal order.

The answer, it would seem, is that Fitzgerald had only the choice of two evils. Had he not dated it out of sequence, he would have had to place it—whether dated or not—within the nine or ten days between the Buchanans' dinner and Gatsby's first party. The effective present of the story, the sense that Nick is narrating the events as he experiences them, is so strong in the novel that were there no calendar reference during Myrtle's party, the reader would inevitably believe that it occurred on the Sunday in June between the dinner party and Nick's first attendance at Gatsby's. As a result, the first three chapters would have taken place within perhaps ten days and would have validated exactly the impression Nick goes to some pains to deny—"that the events of three nights several weeks apart were all that absorbed me"

(p. 37). Perhaps equally significant is the following manuscript passage from the opening of the first chapter: ". . . in telling the story of that summer on Long Island I shall let him [Gatsby] drift into it casually, as he did in life, without suspicion that he would come to dominate it" (MS, p. 3).

The passage is canceled, but, in my judgment, because of its rather clumsy narrative self-consciousness, not because of its attitudes. For it seems that one of the essential qualities of the experience Nick undergoes is that he is surprised to learn in the experiencing itself that it is critical. That Nick comes to realize that Gatsby is "worth the whole damn bunch put together" (p. 103) and after the murder finds himself "on Gatsby's side—and alone" (p. 109) are moral positions that have their full significance only because, as late as the ride to Manhattan, Nick thinks of him as "simply the proprietor of an elaborate road-house next door" (p. 42). To have immersed Nick at once in the affairs of Gatsby and the Buchanans would have undermined a necessary dimension of his experience, and to avoid this, Fitzgerald spaced his first three episodes over "several weeks."

The narrative effects Fitzgerald intended seem to have demanded both that Myrtle's party be an element in building our anticipation of Gatsby's appearance and also that it be reasonably distant from the start of the history of the summer. Perhaps he might have been able to meet both demands by making Gatsby's party somewhat later and Myrtle's somewhat earlier and in chronological order. Obviously he chose not to. Conceivably, keeping Gatsby offstage even longer might have created greater problems, especially after our glimpse of him on the night of the Buchanans' dinner. Certainly, some substantial rewriting would have been necessitated—for the dating of Gatsby's party, for example—and there is no evidence of substantial rewriting in any of the drafts of the book simply to correct its chronology.

One can understand in fairly close detail why the second chapter was placed out of sequence, but to understand in terms of the history and exigency of composition is not to justify as a legitimate artistic means. In fact, the evidences suggest that Fitzgerald may have misplaced the chapter and then consciously tried to disguise the misplacement. Admittedly, there are many temporal discrepancies in *Gatsby* that are clearly inadvertances, but it is difficult to believe that Fitzgerald moved Myrtle's party from one side of Gatsby's party to the other and added both Catherine's mention of Gatsby and the Fourth of July reference— all during the same stage of composition, in the typescript version—and yet failed to realize the contradiction. Even in the kindest interpretation, one must conclude that by making Myrtle's party the second chapter in sequential experience but not in time, he created a narrative dilemma for himself, and failed to resolve it.

Chapter 3 (Gatsby's First Party)

The third chapter opens with a section on Nick's observation of the parties at Gatsby's prior to his invitation. Since he comments on what occurs "at least once a fortnight" (p. 6), a month or more of observation seems indicated, and this suits well enough with Nick's having come east "in the spring of twenty-two" (p. 2) and with a number of other early references to Gatsby's playing Trimalchio. Catherine, for instance, claims, during Myrtle's party, to have been to Gatsby's "about a month ago" (p. 21), or in very late May or early June. Jordan's mention of Gatsby during the dinner party hints that she has already been to his parties, thus, earlier than the first week in June; and the hint is corroborated here in chapter 3 when she and the girls in yellow remember having met "here about a month ago" (p. 28), or in mid-May. Actually, since Jordan speaks of Gatsby's having "once" told her of his attendance at Oxford (p. 32), she seems to have been to his parties a number of times.

The girls in yellow also establish the dating of the party in chapter 3. They tell Jordan they are "sorry you didn't win," and Nick immediately orients the reference: "That was for the golf tournament. She had lost in the finals the week before" (p. 28). Since it is "*the* golf tournament," it is the one in which Jordan played the day after the Buchanans' dinner, and thus, the present party is about a week later, in mid-June. Actually, since the dinner seems to have been on a weekday—Gatsby's house is dark and apparently without guests (p. 14)—and the party on a Saturday (p. 27, et al.), a gap of about ten days might be more exact.[14]

In a general way, this dating of Gatsby's party is corroborated by two references in the closing chapters: in chapter 8, on the morning of the murder, Nick recalls his first attendance at Gatsby's "three months ago" (p. 103); and in chapter 9, at the funeral, he remembers meeting Owl Eyes at the same party, again "three months before" (p. 117). As will be discussed, the relevant period is somewhat less than a literal three months in each case, for Fitzgerald (and Nick) is using the time references to evoke the sense of the completion of the summer. Exactly the same purpose is served by Nick's harking back, in chapter 7 on the night of Myrtle's death, to the dinner party at the Buchanans' "three months before" (p. 97). Evidently, in Fitzgerald's imagination, both nights are early enough events and close enough in time that either might properly evoke the initiation of Nick's summer experience.

Fitzgerald had planned from the first to use the golf tournament to date Gatsby's first party. In the manuscript version, the reference is somewhat stronger because Jordan wins the tournament, the girls in yellow congratulate her, Nick recalls reading about it "a week before" (MS, p. 43), and he and Jordan stop "at frequent intervals while Miss Baker was congratulated on her feat of a week before" (MS, p. 44).

The dating of the party remains firm enough in the final text, but canceling Jordan's victory is part of a curious process of revision that lessens her celebrity and creates an occasional narrative weakness. In the text of the novel, Nick recalls having seen Jordan in "many rotogravure pictures of the sporting life at Asheville and Hot Springs and Palm Beach" (p. 13), yet over the course of the summer she seems always to be in the New York area. It is even a bit surprising that she is staying in East Egg and sleeping as late as 8:00 when she has a trip of forty or fifty miles to her tournament "over in Westchester" (p. 13), on the next day.[15] In the manuscript version, she plays golf with Nick during the Warwick party (MS, p. 122) and is absent from Gatsby's second party—and missed by Nick—because she "was off somewhere playing in a tournament" (MS, p. 51).[16]

The matter is quite a small one, although weakening any strand of verisimilitude bears against the maintenance of the fictive illusion to some degree. More interesting is the general implication that positing a character's existence over a period of time—Jordan's during the summer—and failing to provide or even imply a particular kind of action within that period—her being elsewhere than New York—suggests that the character did not perform that action. Fitzgerald's narrative method in *Gatsby*, which deliberately posits only a few "selected incidents," is especially vulnerable to such suggestion, and it will occur again, far more significantly, in the characterization of Nick.

There are also significant chronological problems connected with Jordan's interview with Gatsby at the party and with the Warwick section that closes chapter 3. Both, however, can be more profitably discussed in connection with the correlating passages in chapter 4. Only one minor matter in the central section of chapter 3 remains to be discussed. At the party, Vladimir Tostoff's *Jazz History of the World* is introduced by the orchestra leader as having "attracted so much attention to Carnegie Hall last May" (p. 33), which, in Gatsby's world of ephemeral sensations, must mean May of 1922, not 1921. Yet, since it is June of 1922, this is a strangely unidiomatic way to refer to "last month" (or to "May of last year," for that matter). It is an extremely minor concern, but it is mentioned here because it is the first of a number of such unidiomatic time references, which, cumulatively at least, have some significance.

The concluding section of chapter 3 opens with a transitional passage which has already been referred to, but which requires full examination because it relates critically to a number of aspects of the novel's use of time and its narrative method:

> Reading over what I have written so far, I see I have given the impression that the events of three nights several weeks apart were all that absorbed me. On the contrary, they were merely casual events in a crowded summer, and, until much later, they absorbed me infinitely less than my personal affairs.
>
> (p. 37)[17]

First, it should be reiterated how misleading the reference back to the "three nights" is. What Nick as author and we as readers have just read over is the departure of Gatsby's guests from his first party, while the host looks on, "his hand up in a formal gesture of farewell" (p. 37). But that scene is neither "several weeks" into the history of the summer—in fact it is perhaps ten days after the Buchanans' dinner—nor is it, as the "three nights" imply, the third of the major events of that summer history. As has been explained, the "reading over" transition was originally designed to follow and to refer to Myrtle's party, and, in spite of the reshuffling of the incidents, one must still somehow understand the transition to refer to the time of the second chapter if any sense is to be made of where we are in the progress of the summer.

The transition is quite explicitly Nick's intruding as author-narrator into his own narration, and he does so, it should be noted, because he realizes that, by the mere selection of events, he may have suggested a principle of unity—the developing focus on Gatsby's affairs—that was not in fact recognized at the time in the summer of 1922 to which the narration has progressed.

He intrudes to deny that his experience as character possessed this quality at this time; thus, he intrudes to insist that the integrity of his summer experience would be damaged by imposing on its earlier portion insights attained only "much later." The purpose of the intrusion, evidently, is to insist that the integrity of the summer experience requires recreating it temporally as it actually occurred; but the very fact of the intrusion's misplacement itself compromises the integrity it insists upon. It is a remarkable incoherence.

The temporal difficulties noted thus far are, from one point of view, merely the ramifications of the misplacement of Myrtle's party, rather than separate and distinct incoherences. Such, however, is not the case with the balance of chapter 3 that the "reading over" transition introduces: the materials on Nick's working and studying, his wanderings in "the enchanted metropolitan twilight," and the beginnings of his romance with Jordan, including the house party at Warwick.

It may be profitable to investigate these first within a context somewhat larger and vaguer than strict chronology, that of more general narrative intentions, such as temporal impression. Simply on the basis of this closing section, one can hardly deny that temporal impression was a matter of conscious concern to Fitzgerald, even though the detailed chronology that documents it ordinarily was not, as has already become apparent.

In terms of general intentions, then, Fitzgerald obviously is using Nick's authorial intrusion to mark the end of the novel's first movement. This, in turn, coincides with the end of the first part of the summer, the references to "so far," "several weeks," and "much later" establishing this temporal impression. Then, the pace of the narration is for a time slowed by leaving the main line of action—the progress of Gatsby's affairs—and adverting to Nick's experience. But Nick's doings also are intended to have positive narrative value of their own: the paragraphs on the romance with Jordan carry forward the major subplot, and both they and the materials on Nick's working and roaming the twilight city would seem designed to contribute significantly to his characterization by establishing a sense of what his experience is apart from his involvement with Gatsby and the Buchanans.

This latter narrative intention is all but explicitly stated in Nick's insistence that during the early part of the summer, Gatsby's affairs "absorbed me infinitely less than my personal affairs." Somewhat more indirectly, Nick also claims that his summer was "crowded" with "casual events," which is a different emphasis, although it can be accommodated within the larger intention of presenting a Nick who has purposes and concerns of his own. Most of what immediately follows on Nick's working, becoming acquainted with his fellow bond salesmen, and studying at the Yale Club seems keyed rather more to developing a summer crowded with casual events, since the actions sound like summerlong routines and are a good deal more muted than one would expect of absorbing personal affairs. "Most of the time I worked" (p. 37), says Nick, and indeed, he seems, by and large, simply busy.

He does, however, and in the midst of this material, report having had "a short affair" with a girl from Jersey City. This is unarguably a "personal affair," and, since it ends "when she went on her vacation in July," at least part of it belongs to the early part of the summer when Nick was too self-absorbed to pay much notice to the three nights that brought him into Gatsby's story. But quite oddly, the affair is narrated with no more impression of emotional engagement than Nick's lunching with his co-workers or avoiding the "rioters" at the Yale Club; when the girl leaves, he "let it blow quietly away" (p. 37).

The emotional tone changes strikingly, however, with the next two paragraphs on Nick's wanderings. These are highly lyrical and evocative, presenting a Nick who responds to "the racy, adventurous feel of the city," and aches for involvement in it. He spins romantic fantasies about women he sees on the street; he feels the same "haunting loneliness" that he perceives in "poor young clerks," loitering and "wasting the most poignant moments of night and life"; and he watches theatergoing couples in their taxis, "a sinking in my heart. . . . Imagining I, too, was hurrying toward gayety and sharing their intimate excitement" (p. 38).

It is difficult to see any of this as coming under the rubric of the absorbing personal affairs of Nick's early summer, or even as the events of a crowded summer, for the emotions that are elicited are those of longing, even of deprivation, not those of engagement. Insofar as this crepuscular lyricism has a narrative justification, presumably it is to establish Nick's "romantic readiness" (to vary his own term) for the relationship with Jordan that occupies the last several paragraphs of chapter 3.

This is introduced by Nick's "For a while I lost sight of Jordan Baker, and then in midsummer I found her again," and progresses through a number of stages marked by a number of emotional responses. "At first," Nick says, "I was flattered to go places with her"; then he feels "something more . . . a sort of tender curiosity" (p. 38); finally, during the "careless driver" conversation at Warwick, "for a moment I thought I loved her" (p. 39). Yet in spite of this content, and very much in contrast to the lyricism of the lonely wanderings immediately before, the tone of the section on the romance with Jordan is emotionally quite cool. Nick announces various feelings, but there is no evocation of intensity, enchantment, relief, fulfillment, exhilaration, or heightened sensibility. When he discovers her incurable dishonesty, he is "casually sorry, and then I forgot"; and when he thinks "for a moment" he loves her, he pulls himself up short and worries about extricating himself from "that tangle back home" with the girl with the "faint mustache of perspiration" (p. 39).

At best, these materials that close chapter 3 barely fulfill the immediate narrative requirement of detailing Nick's summer crowded with casual events or his absorption in his personal affairs during the early part of the summer. Only the twilight yearnings seem emotionally absorbing, and these bespeak an emptiness that can hardly qualify even as casual event. Accordingly, the larger narrative purpose of Nick's characterization is also less than well served, since the variations in tone very curiously suggest that his feelings are most fully engaged by the sweet, sad loneliness of roaming the city. And since the variations in tone correspond to various of Nick's relationships with women, even more curiously, his romantic fantasies about women he hasn't met seem more intense than either his affair with the girl from Jersey City or his incipient romance with Jordan. In context, the emotional evocation of the twilight wanderings section seems self-indulgent, since it works at cross-purposes to establishing a Nick with sufficient affairs of his own to be occupied or with a sufficient inner life of his own to justify the uses which the novel will make of his character.

Thus far, this closing section of the chapter 3 has been investigated with regard simply to the nature and quality of the actions, the narrative intentions they seem designed to serve, and their less than total success in doing so. Little has been said about time, and nothing about chronology. Yet there are, of course, temporal references with this material that are as validly part of the fictional assertion as what Nick had for lunch or where he strolled in Manhattan; and there are temporal intimations which are, at least formally, as relevant as the connotations of emotional intensity or relaxation.

This is to approach the basic fictive demand for consistent

chronology. The author is of course free to be relatively precise or imprecise in adverting to the conventions of the clock, the calendar, or the seasons. But once he does choose, he has made a commitment in terms of a narrative discipline he himself has imposed—and imposed, one must think, because it is consonant with values or implications or patternings he wishes his narrative to bear. Virtually nothing of the indications of time in this closing of chapter 3 is purposeful toward an observable narrative intention; virtually everything complicates and aggravates the problems of coherence already noted.

To begin with, Fitzgerald has designed a miniature chronology—apart from that of the summer of 1922—for the details of both Nick's working and his lonely wandering, that of a single day. We hear that he arrived at work "in the early morning," "lunched" with his co-workers, "took dinner" at the Yale Club, "then" studied for "a conscientious hour," and "after that," strolled about. His yearnings continue the progress of this day: he felt the raciness and adventure of the city "at night"; "at the enchanted metropolitan twilight," he suffered haunting loneliness; and, "again at eight o'clock," his heart sank at the gay and intimate theatergoers.

Since both the working and the yearning are set within this prototypical day, the implication is that the evening's dissatisfactions are virtually as regular as the day's occupations. The pattern would seem to suggest a dichotomized soul, grubbing until dusk and then aching to fill its emptiness—Seiters calls him "Walter Mitty on a busy street"[18]; and the pattern has an odd bit of support in Nick's calling dinner at the Yale Club "the gloomiest event of my day"—a superlative singular that sounds like the most extreme of many similar cases. But the Nick Carraway we meet before and after this section is by no means so schematized nor so melodramatic.

Moreover, we find the report of the affair with the girl from Jersey City embedded within the framework of this dismal day. It is narrated between lunch and dinner, and the girl herself is tied to Nick's place of employment: she "worked in the accounting department." The "short affair" is in the text, I take it, to validate Nick's claim of early absorption in his personal affairs; but it is a singular event, unlike the customary events that surround it. It should belong to the linear chronology of the summer, not the circular chronology of the prototypical day. Yet it shares the joyless tonality of the day; it is narrated as if it is an occurrence that engages no emotion whatever.

This seems to complicate the day's characterization of Nick to one who keeps his nose to the grindstone all day, presses it to the toy shop window each evening, and carries on a "short affair" in the odd moments. The resulting picture has very little to do with the Nick we meet elsewhere in the novel; indeed, it seems to have little to do with any believable human character. It would make greater sense in terms of character for the time of the evening wanderings to be later in the summer than the time of the short affair, and there is one slight hint—in "I *began* to like New York" (italics added)— that it took some time for Nick to develop his twilight melancholy. Still, to insist that such is the case is to ignore the far stronger implication of the day of work and wandering.

The closing section of chapter 3 does, however, contain a good deal of evidence of linear movement through the summer of 1922. The "reading over" transition takes us "several weeks" beyond the Buchanans' dinner and (though with the incoherence that has been noted), rather surely to, or a bit beyond, Myrtle's party "a few days before the Fourth of July." The end of the "short affair"—whether it precedes or is part of the time of Nick's prototypical day—moves us somewhat further; since it ends in July, it all but necessarily ends later than Myrtle's party.

Nick's characteristic day of work and yearning, presented so as to emphasize its repetitiveness, has are only minimal connection to the progress of the summer. Still, the following section on Nick's romance with Jordan begins, "For a while, I lost sight of Jordan Baker," and it is difficult not to identify the "while" of his having lost sight of her with the "while" of his twilight wanderings. In any case, losing sight of Jordan necessarily means the elapsing of some time after she and Nick attended Gatsby's party in mid-June, and the "midsummer" when he "found her again," by the novel's customary usage, should be July, and perhaps mid-July. There is a kind of substantiation for this conclusion in the sense that whether the "short affair" ends before or during the wanderings, both must be earlier than Nick's finding Jordan again.

The romance's developing emotions have been explored, and the implication of time elapsing as they develop is supported by the use of temporal indicators. Nick is flattered to be seen with her "at first," "then" feels a tender curiosity, and, "one day," at Warwick, learns the secret of her affectation and discovers her incurable dishonesty. There is, throughout the closing of chapter 3, from the "reading over" intrusion to the end of the chapter, abundant indication of the elapsing of time: actions that seem unlikely or impossible to be performed at the same time are narrated; these actions are significantly varied in emotional tonality; during the romance with Jordan, Nick goes through a series of different attitudes that are keyed to different times by the use of temporal indicators.

There is not much in the way of adversion to the calendar, however: the intrusion is "several weeks" into the summer; the short affair ends in July; Nick finds Jordan again "in midsummer." But calendar time is elapsing, and transposing the chronological indications and impressions must require that Nick finds Jordan again at some time in July and that their romance continues for at least a couple of weeks before the house party at Warwick. These are quite minimal assumptions, perhaps even too minimal for the diverse quality of Nick's experience that the closing of chapter 3 presents. But even on this basis, the closing of chapter 3 will account for most of the month of July 1922, and no other events of the same period seem to be presented anywhere else in the novel.

At this point, it might be profitable to refer back to the general strategic purposes of this closing section of chapter 3 in terms of the structuring and pacing of the novel. It marks the closing of the first movement of the novel and then slows the narrative pace by leaving Gatsby's affairs, which will be resumed with chapter 4. This latter quality of the narrative has been persuasively analyzed by Eble. He notes, for example, the static quality of the reunion scene in chapter 5 at the exact center of the book, the "deliberate pause" with the opening of the following chapter, and the regained momentum of the Plaza chapter; and he aptly characterizes the effect of the entire narrative as "a pattern of movement and withdrawal."[19]

The closing section of chapter 3 is so clearly a moment of withdrawal that it is sometimes spoken of as if progress through the summer of 1922 has been arrested. Bruccoli, for example, says that Fitzgerald relocated the section "to convey the impression of the passage of time."[20] The opening of this section might well convey such an idea, as Nick as narrator intrudes to take us out of the time frame of the summer and into the time of the narration itself, and then seems to promise a retrospective look at his own activities during the period of the "three nights." But once we hear of the affair with the girl from Jersey City, we have not merely the impression of the passage of time, but also the accounting for the passage of time; and a considerable, if relatively unspecified, amount of it has passed when the chapter closes with the "careless driver" conversation.

With the comparable moment of withdrawal that Eble noted in the beginning of chapter 6, the matter is less complicated because Nick as narrator leaves the time frame of the summer for a completely different time frame, that of Gatsby's years with Dan Cody, and, once there, he stays there. But in chapter 3, the experience of Nick as character exists in the same time as Gatsby's plan to win Daisy. A considerable amount of event and a considerable passage of time occurs for Nick, while Gatsby, who was been kept waiting in the wings for what seems only a few pages of text, is being required to do nothing for better than a month after finding a means of reunion with Daisy.

I would submit that a "moment of withdrawal" achieved at the cost of the elapsing of about a third of the total time frame while the characteristically energetic and resolute hero remains inert is something less than a narrative masterstroke.

Chapter 4 (Lunch with Wolfsheim)

The fourth chapter presents an extremely large number of chronological problems, many of which derive from Fitzgerald's revision. It is less a matter, I think, of chapter 4 being especially carelessly written than that, by this point in the novel, a number of narrative (and hence chronological) strands come together, many with less than complete coherence. Most of the chapter deals with the events of a single, critical day in Nick's summer, but its first elements exist apart from the main plot line.

The chapter opens with an odd time reference: "On Sunday morning while church bells rang in villages along-shore, the world and its mistress returned to Gatsby's house and twinkled hilariously on his lawn." Then, after a brief paragraph on Gatsby's guests gossiping about him, the narrative moves to another time and Nick's compilation of the guest list: "Once I wrote down . . ." (p. 40). Since the actions of the opening paragraphs are customary, not particular, "Sunday morning"—rather than "Sunday mornings" or "every Sunday morning"—seems purposeless and, again, oddly unidiomatic. It is even momentarily confusing, since it may seem to specify the Sunday after the Saturday of Nick's first attendance at Gatsby's. It will be recalled that as Nick leaves, Gatsby reminds him, "And don't forget we're

going up in the hydroplane tomorrow morning at nine o'clock"
(p. 35).

Then follows the guest list, written "on the empty spaces of a
timetable . . . headed 'This schedule in effect July 5, 1922'" (p.
40).[21] Since it is written on such unlikely material, we might
reasonably infer that Nick had no other paper available and, thus,
that he wrote it on the train; and if he had this timetable with
him on the train, we might further infer that he wrote the list
after July 5th. But beyond this, the list is of no use to determining
chronology. The list may seem intended as a device for dating
the action of the chapter, but, logically, Nick could have compiled
it almost any time in July and August. And although it is true
that the subsequent actions of the chapter occur "late in July"
(p. 41), some at least of the closing section of chapter 3 (as has
been demonstrated) must be later than 5 July; and in the manuscript version, the 5 July timetable occurs in conjunction with
the placing of those actions in June (MS, p. 65). Somewhat surprisingly in view of its specificity, Fitzgerald seems not to have
intended the timetable date as a chronological indication; in fact,
it may well simply reflect an actual change of train service to a
summer schedule.[22]

The remaining four events—the ride to Manhattan, the lunch
with Wolfsheim, Jordan's narrative, and the cab ride—all occur
on the same day. Gatsby calls for Nick "at nine o'clock, one morning late in July," and Nick reports that, by this time, "I had gone
to two of his parties, mounted in his hydroplane, and, at his
urgent invitation, made frequent use of his beach" (p. 41).
Shortly thereafter, he adds, "I had talked with him perhaps six
times in the past month" (p. 42), and, at tea that afternoon, Jordan
says that, "about six weeks ago" (p. 51), Daisy heard Gatsby's
name for the first time in years when she herself mentioned
him at the dinner party in chapter 1. The coincidence of these
references is acceptable, but not exact. If it is a month since
Nick's first party at Gatsby's, it should be mid-July, not late July.
Further, six weeks from the dinner party should take us only to
about July 20th, a little early to be considered late in the month.
Still, Nick's "month" is clearly a round figure, and Jordan's
"about six weeks" literally an approximation; thus, there is no
real contradiction.

The temporal location of this chapter was quite different in
manuscript. There, Gatsby calls "at nine o'clock one morning in
June" (MS, p. 65), and Jordan adverts to the dinner party as "not
three weeks ago" (MS, p. 90), putting the action around 25 June.

The typescript version changed the time to late July and added Nick's claim of having talked to Gatsby perhaps six times in the past month (both as in the final text), but the typescript also has Jordan refer to the dinner party as "about a month ago" (Gal., 24), which would have put the action in early, not late July. Fitzgerald corrected this last reference to "about six weeks ago" in his revision of the galleys, and thus achieved the relative accuracy of the published text.

The movement of this chapter forward in time is quite interesting and will be examined later. But there is a smaller and curious matter that might well be explored here: Nick's claim in both manuscript and final text to have attended two of Gatsby's parties. In the manuscript time frame, Nick is referring to his attendance at two parties within two weeks or less, which would seem to necessitate including his attendance at the party in chapter 3. In the final version, in part because Nick says he has spoken with Gatsby six times in the past month, substantially the same language seems to indicate two parties in addition to the first. The change here introduced no incoherence into the final text, but it is usefully illustrative of how Fitzgerald's relocation of events often altered the implication of those events.

This alteration of implication is much more troublesome when applied to Gatsby's actions and motives. In the manuscript version, he enlists Jordan and arranges that the proposed reunion with Daisy be presented to Nick within two weeks of first meeting him, and his haste appears to be evidence of his devotion. In the published text, he seems quite careful and circumspect in cultivating Nick before allowing the proposal to be broached; he seems this way because he waits about five weeks, from mid-June to late July. One may argue that Gatsby's circumspection in the final text is also evidence of devotion to Daisy; but, since the manuscript version contains the same proposal made the same way, and even after the same cultivating of Nick, it seems problematical whether it is the author or the reader who is supplying the hero's motivation.

As I suggested earlier, five weeks of circumspection seems much out of character for the resolute Gatsby. Further, the change in time scheme requires the incurably dishonest Jordan to keep her pledge of silence for these five weeks, even though for some part of them she and Nick are dating. This is the same Jordan, it will be remembered, who, on first meeting Nick, eavesdrops "unashamed" (p. 10) on the Buchanans' quarrel and advises Nick that Tom has a mistress, and who, on her second meeting with him, notes publicly that the girl in yellow has dyed her hair and tells Nick that she disbelieves Gatsby's claim of having attended Oxford. The relocation of the chapter in time causes problems for both characterizations, for Fitzgerald demonstrates too little sense that what they do is significantly modified by when they do it.

As has been mentioned, Fitzgerald included in the original verison of the lunch with Wolfsheim the reappearance of Myrtle in Tom's company at the Forty-Second Street restaurant. As a matter of fact, the statement at the opening of chapter 2 in the published text—that Tom "turned up in popular restaurants with her and, leaving her at a table, sauntered about, chatting with whomsoever he knew" (pp. 15–16)—is exactly what occurs in the manuscript version of chapter 4. Clearly Fitzgerald reworked the incident into the composition of his chapter on Myrtle's party.

Myrtle had first appeared in the original version of chapter 4, straining and leering at the gas pump when Gatsby's then-chauffeured car stopped on the way to Manhattan, so her reappearance was a rather outrageous coincidence that was well excised. With it, however, went almost all of Tom's expostulations to Nick for not having called. In the manuscript, Tom goes on for some time, lecturing Nick on his culpability, his insensitivity to Daisy's feelings, even his violation of basic decencies. Since his mistress is waiting at the table, Tom's moral hectoring is delightfully hypocritical, having much of the "transition from libertine to prig" (p. 87) that Nick remarks during the Plaza scene, and evoking a mock contrite promise that Nick will call "this week sure" (MS, p. 84).[23]

All of this was cut in revision except for Tom's opening line "Where've you been? . . . Daisy's furious because you haven't called up" (p. 49), which causes difficulty since it sounds as if Nick has been out of touch with the Buchanans for as long as six or seven weeks—about half the summer—and since Daisy is anything but furious when Nick does call on the next day. In the manuscript version it is clear that Nick, somewhat repelled by the dinner party, has indeed been out of touch in the meanwhile—for two weeks or so. But by tripling the interval and retaining the same complaint, Fitzgerald has required the reader either to ignore the temporal implications of the narrative or to create for himself some strangely unreported meeting and subsequent avoidance in the interim.

Jordan's narrative is more relevant to a consideration of the chronology of the novel's past, but her account of the conversation with Gatsby at the party creates yet another problem. Astoundingly, her account clearly implies that, at the time Gatsby decides to use Nick's house as a setting for the reunion, he does not know that Nick is Daisy's cousin. It would of course be absurd for Gatsby to presume that Daisy Fay Buchanan of Louisville, Lake Forest, and East Egg would accept the invitation of a total stranger to have tea at his "weatherbeaten cardboard bungalow" (p. 2), and, beyond doubt, this cannot be Fitzgerald's intention. Rather the absurd implication is the result of the narrative's lack of control of the sense of when Gatsby learns and when he intends certain things.

According to Jordan's account, after buying his house to be just across the bay from Daisy and giving his parties half in expectation that she would wander in, "Then he began asking people casually if they knew her, and I was the first one he found" (p. 52). The literal statement of the text is that Gatsby "found" Jordan—that is, became aware she knows Daisy—"first" and, therefore, before he "found" Nick, whom we know he invited "early that Saturday morning" (p. 27), and who, in these terms, would have been "found" if Gatsby knew he was Daisy's cousin. Thus, his finding Jordan, whom Gatsby already knows, would appear to mean that he became aware of her acquaintance with Daisy only on the night of the party itself. This last inference is supported by enough detail that it appears to be Fitzgerald's conscious intention.

Jordan's statement that she "was the first one he found" is immediately followed by "it was that night he sent for me at his dance" (p. 42), in which the logical antecedent of "it" is Gatsby's finding her. So, too, the circumstances of his summons argue. Although Gatsby is seated with Jordan when he first meets Nick, at about "midnight" (p. 31), and stands "alone" (p. 33) and apparently at ease while the *Jazz History* is performed, he summons Jordan unexpectedly enough to evoke her "astonishment" (p. 33), and quite late even for one of his parties; for immediately after she leaves, Nick says, "I was alone and it was almost two" (p. 34). And Gatsby keeps her in conversation for "about an hour" (p. 35). It seems that we are indeed intended to understand that he learned of Jordan's acquaintance with Daisy only during the party.

If this judgment is allowed, incidentally, one might well note the stark contrast between the Gatsby who, immediately upon discovering that Jordan knows Daisy, urgently summons her to a

2:00 A.M. meeting and at once enlists her in his plan to regain
his lost love, and the Gatsby who waits patiently for five weeks
before allowing the same plan to be revealed to Nick.

Yet by the account Jordan gives of their conversation, it is Nick,
not she, whom Gatsby wants for an intermediary. Nick poses just
this question: "Why didn't he ask you to arrange a meeting?";
Jordan replies, "He wants her to see his house . . . and your house
is right next door." Nick's great attraction for Gatsby is, to be
sure, his proximity, from which Gatsby easily can, and does, display his credentials as suitor. But Gatsby seems to have decided
to utilize Nick's house before the beginning of his conversation
with Jordan, and, therefore, it would appear, before he learns of
Nick's relationship to Daisy. Jordan reports:

> . . . and you should have heard the elaborate way he worked up to
> it. Of course, I immediately suggested a luncheon in New York—and
> I thought he'd go mad:
>   "I don't want to do anything out of the way!" he kept saying. "I
> want to see her right next door."
>
> (p. 52)

In the face of the evidence of the text, one cannot explain away
the difficulty by supposing that Jordan herself tells Gatsby of
Nick and Daisy's relationship. In terms of the text Fitzgerald has
in fact written—rather than what we think he ought to have written or would have intended—Jordan cannot tell him because
there is no time for her to do so. Since Gatsby summons Jordan
to talk about Daisy, clearly they do not discuss who her cousins
may be before "he worked up to it." Nor does such a discussion
precede Jordan's suggesting—not just "immediately," but "of
course . . . immediately"—a luncheon in New York. As soon as
the topic of Daisy is broached, Jordan "immediately" suggests,
and Gatsby, with obviously equal immediacy, rejects. Thus the
immediate rejection must be based on a determination "to see
her right next door" that precedes the conversation. But "right
next door" means Nick, and Nick can be of value only if Gatsby
knows he is Daisy's cousin. It is necessary that Gatsby know, but
the time references insist it is impossible.[24]

Further, if Gatsby is not ignorant of Nick and Daisy's relationship, it is difficult to see why he broaches the matter to Jordan
rather than to Nick. One might wish to argue Nick's greater moral
scrupulosity, but Gatsby, who has met Nick only two hours earlier, can hardly know this. Still, Gatsby's selection of Jordan

rather than Nick is merely part of the larger problem of his select-
ing Jordan at all: to choose her as an intermediary to Nick has,
at this point in time, very little narrative coherence. This party
is actually only the second time Nick has met Jordan, and, although it may be insisted that Gatsby is ignorant of that fact and
does indeed meet Nick in her company, Jordan has in fact been
escorted by another man—the "persistent undergraduate" (p.
29)—and casual pairings are the order of the day at Gatsby's
parties. It is a close question whether the narrative supplies less
reason for Gatsby's choosing Nick as intermediary to Daisy or for
his choosing Jordan as intermediary to Nick. There is nothing to
explain why at this time he should think either or both would
be of aid to him, because the sense in the novel of exactly when
things occur is so weak.

The fourth chapter closes with Nick's ride with Jordan in the
victoria; he says: "Unlike Gatsby and Tom Buchanan, I had no
girl whose disembodied face floated along the dark cornices and
blinding signs, and so I drew up the girl beside me, tightening
my arms. Her wan, scornful mouth smiled, and so I drew her up
again closer, this time to my face" (p. 53). This passage and the
"careless driver" conversation in chapter 3 are the only scenes
of intimacy between Nick and Jordan, and, therefore, they are
crucial to the portrayal, and the chronology, of their romance.

The ride in the victoria occurs on the same day as the ride to
Manhattan, and thus "late in July." But the romance seems at a
very early stage: on the ride to Manhattan, Nick asks whether
Gatsby is in love with Jordan with no hint of possessiveness,
jealousy, or even relief when Gatsby says, "No" (p. 44). And the
kiss in the victoria, which one suspects is their first kiss from
the very fact that it is narrated,[25] seems to present an uncommit-
ted, even opportunistic, Nick. Emotionally, the romance seems
to have a long way to go, yet, since it ends in effect on the evening
of Myrtle's death, at the very end of August, the five weeks or so
Fitzgerald allows for it seems much too short.

The matter is much complicated by the Warwick section in
chapter 3. There, it will be recalled, we learn of Nick's "short
affair with a girl who lived in Jersey City," which ended "when
she went on her vacation in July"; of his finding Jordan again "in
midsummer," after losing sight of her "for a while" (p. 38); and,
finally, of the early stages of their romance, culminating in the
"careless driver" conversation at Warwick.

One can only guess at how to translate this evidence to the
calendar, but it seems to require the passage of a good deal of

time. It is specified that the Jersey City affair ends in July; his losing sight of Jordan "for a while" accounts for some time after Gatsby's first party in mid-June; his finding her again "in mid-summer," by Fitzgerald's customary usage, should indicate mid-July; and the stages of growing involvement with Jordan require the elapsing of some significant period of time after Nick "found her again." To make sense of these impressions, the Warwick house party should occur no earlier than very late July or very early August. Yet, as with the cab ride passage, too little time would be left—now perhaps only three or four weeks—for the romance with Jordan to be of the continuance and seriousness the novel requires. The matter is further aggravated by the requirement of later chapters that Nick spend at least part of three different weekends in August separated from Jordan: the Sunday that Tom and Sloane visit Gatsby's, the following Saturday, when Tom and Daisy attend Gatsby's party, and another Saturday, when Nick goes over to see why the lights are out at Gatsby's.

More importantly, however, the Warwick passage and the cab ride must correlate in time, for they are parts of the same romance between the same people during the same summer. And although there is no direct reference between them, and although the cab ride is narrated later, it must apparently be earlier. It is hard to see how else to make sense of Nick's opportunism during the cab ride and his thinking he is in love during Warwick. Certainly, one cannot suppose that the romance progresses from the verge of complete commitment at Warwick, then to casual dalliance on the cab ride, and finally to the wrenching renunciation of the last chapter.

There is no need to think of Nick's behavior during the cab ride as especially culpable: he is exploratory and perhaps even mildly predatory. Jordan's attraction at the moment is not that she is the girl "whose disembodied face floated" in Nick's imagination; she is not; she is "the girl beside me" (p. 53), the girl who happens to be there. She is something far more important after the conversation at Warwick when she "shifted our relationship and for a moment I thought I loved her" (p. 39).[26]

If Nick's romance is to be responded to as the story of a developing human relationship, then somehow the reader must locate in his understanding the cab ride in chapter 4 before the Warwick house party in chapter 3, although there is nothing in the text to invite him to do so. Quite to the contrary, the cab ride is specifically located on the same day as the ride to Manhattan, the lunch with Wolfsheim, and Jordan's narration. This very fact necessitates the reader's thinking of the cab ride as occurring "now" in the progress of the summer—that is, at that point in time to which chapter 4 has proceeded beyond chapter 3, in which the Warwick passage occurs.

Again, the manner of Fitzgerald's composition has exacerbated the problem. Chapter 4, and the kiss in the victoria, was written first, and, at the time of its composition, the events of the day were located in "June" (MS, p. 65) and—two pages before the account of the cab ride—"not three weeks" (MS, p. 90) after Nick meets Jordan at the Buchanans'. The impression in the published text that this is their first kiss—which makes little sense if it happens after the careless driver conversation and thus late in July or early in August—was obviously the intention of the manuscript version.

As has been explained, the Warwick passage was originally the ending of the Myrtle's party chapter (the fourth to be written), which Fitzgerald composed only after writing the earliest version of the chapter that presents the lunch with Wolfsheim and the kiss in the victoria (the third written). But when Myrtle's party became the second chapter in the typescript version, the Warwick section, preceded by the "reading over what I have written so far" transition, was moved to the close of the third chapter, in which Gatsby's first party is narrated.[27]

Insofar as he had a sense of its location, Fitzgerald seems always to have intended the Warwick weekend to be at least as late as mid-July; so the ending of the Jersey City affair and the finding Jordan in midsummer argue. But his reshuffling events placed it in the text before the cab ride, which was written earlier and which was originally intended to occur earlier. The result is contradiction between the tonality of the kiss in the victoria and the momentum of the narrative's effective present. It may well be noted that when Fitzgerald originally wrote, in the Warwick section, of Nick's losing sight of Jordan "for a while" (MS, p. 120), it was for a while after the kiss in the victoria, not, as in the final text, for a while after the party at Gatsby's. The original scheme arranged the events in Nick's relationship with Jordan—the dinner, the party, the cab ride, and his finding her again—in a temporal order appropriate to their increasing intensity. Fitzgerald's reversal of the last two in revision creates a crucial incoherence.

The two remaining references to Nick's romance may be conveniently handled here, but neither adds to our knowledge. In chapter 6, on the day of Tom and Sloane's visit to Gatsby's, Nick says that "For several weeks, . . . mostly I was in New York, trotting around with Jordan" (p. 67). The visit occurs in August, although, as will be seen, the narrative is self-contradictory about when in August. Thus, the "trotting around" tells us nothing new; it merely emphasizes the romance's consuming a good deal of Nick's time and energy. So, too, the reference in chapter 8 to Jordan's frequent calls to Nick at the office (p. 103) merely adds to our impression of a well-established and continuing relationship. It is this impression that what little we have of chronology tends to undermine by seeming to huddle together the details of Nick's romance into too little calendar time for the relationship to have the significance it requires.

There are two further problems with the Warwick episode, the first of which is again the result of revision. When Jordan lies about leaving the borrowed car in the rain, Nick recalls the scandal of her cheating, which had eluded his memory on the evening of the dinner at the Buchanans'. The psychology of his remembering is nicely convincing, but not the timing: it takes Nick perhaps six or seven weeks—just about half the summer— to remember.

Much of the Warwick episode is in fact a reworking, and an improvement, of the original version of Jordan's behavior toward Nick at Gatsby's first party. In the manuscript Jordan is far more inviting to Nick; in fact, she sounds a bit like Mae West when she tells him, "You appeal to me" (MS, p. 48). Shortly thereafter, she explains that she likes men who are "straightshooters" (MS, p. 51), as Nick is, although she is not one herself. It is this admission that triggers his recall of the story of her cheating. The "straightshooter" conversation is clearly the ancestor of the careless driver conversation at Warwick, and, although on every other score the revision is a great improvement, realistically it makes far better sense for Nick to remember the story ten days, not six weeks, after it first eluded him. As happens so often in these opening chapters, Fitzgerald has weakened an element of his narrative by uprooting an incident from its original temporal setting and relocating it in a new setting to which it is incongruent.

The last of these problems has to do with Nick's resolution after the careless driver conversation "to get myself definitely out of that tangle back home" with the girl with the "faint mustache of perspiration" (p. 39). In chapter 1, he had reported that gossip about the relationship "was one of the reasons I came East" (p. 14), so it is rather strange that he has allowed the tangle to persist so long, and stranger the later one thinks of the location of the Warwick party. Far stranger, however, is that Nick's affair with the girl from Jersey City roused no such scruples.

Chapter 5 (The Reunion)

Except for a little pointless ambiguity, the narrative locates the events of chapter 5 firmly enough. The chapter opens with the conversation in which Nick agrees to invite Daisy to tea and Gatsby offers him an unspecified opportunity in selling bonds. The conversation takes place "that night"—that is, the night of the lunch with Wolfsheim. Thus, Nick's offer to call Daisy "tomorrow" and invite her for "the day after tomorrow" (p. 54) refers to the two days immediately following the lunch with Wolfsheim.

The narrative then becomes somewhat vague because Gatsby responds to Nick's initial offer by insisting "I don't want to put you to any trouble," and to his further offer to "put it off for a few days" (p. 54) by worrying about the condition of Nick's lawn. Nick does indeed phone Daisy "next morning," but the day of his tea party, and the reunion, is specified only as "the day agreed upon" (p. 55).

The best inference available is that Nick—and perhaps Fitzgerald—thinks of the somewhat incoherent conversation with Gatsby as having constituted an agreement. There is no better corroboration in the final text than Gatsby's allusion on the evening of the reunion to the financial offer as "what I proposed the other night" (p. 60), which would be reasonable enough for a reference back about forty hours in time. In his revision of the book's galleys, however, Fitzgerald did insert, and then cancel, a line for Nick in the opening conversation: "Now, we've agreed, have we, on the day after tomorrow?"[28] The cancellation casts some doubt on the significance of the line, but I take it to be Fitzgerald's momentary attempt to clarify the time sequence, which he then struck out because it extends the conversation unprofitably.

What vagueness there is in the final text about exactly when the reunion occurs derives ultimately from the revision of the manuscript's dating: "The day we had set was the third of July and pouring rain" (MS, p. 125).[29] With the movement in the typescript version of the events of chapter 4 to late July, the calendar reference became inappropriate, and the sentence was collapsed to "The day agreed upon was pouring rain" (p. 55).

There are in the manuscript only two exact calendar datings of summer events, and neither survived beyond that stage of composition. In the case in point, the deletion left only referential detail, and that detail is somewhat less firm than one might wish. As a result, although it does seem that Fitzgerald wanted to place the reunion exactly two days after lunch, the final text does not definitively locate it. In any case, there are no grounds for thinking the reunion can be more than a few days later, and the difference is quite immaterial to further investigation. Thus, in spite of a little weakness in the evidence of the text, the reunion can be treated as if it had indeed been specified as two days after the lunch with Wolfsheim. The reunion, then, occurs in very late July—two days after the lunch with Wolfsheim, which is itself "late in July." This represents an adjustment forward of three or four weeks from the time of the manuscript version.

The change of location of the reunion looks like part of a general revision that moved a number of events forward from their manuscript dating. The reunion was changed from the third of July to very late July; similarly, the lunch with Wolfsheim went from "June" (MS, p. 65) and "not three weeks" (MS, p. 90) after the Buchanans' dinner, to "late in July" (p. 41) and "about six weeks" (p. 51) after the dinner in the published text.

It is difficult to decide whether Fitzgerald moved Myrtle's party forward as well. In manuscript, it was "several weeks" after the Buchanans' dinner, but within "the early part of the summer" (MS, p. 120); it was also designed to precede the lunch with Wolfsheim, a June event in manuscript. Although one cannot have confidence that Fitzgerald had a clear sense of its location, the evidence does point to an original dating about a week before its final placement "a few days before the Fourth of July" (p. 17). Quite possibly, it may have been related to the Fourth of July because the relocation of chapters 4 and 5 left the narrative with no specific event early in that month.

Fitzgerald may have decided to move all these events forward between the manuscript composition of chapter 5 and chapter 6. As will be investigated in detail later, the major events of chapter 6—Tom and Sloane's visit to Gatsby's, and Gatsby's second party—are located in August in both the manuscript and the later versions. It is possible, however, that he wrote some way into chapter 6 before making this decision, for he crossed out in the manuscript the disappearance of Tom and his friends "around a bend" and wrote in "under the August foliage" (MS, p. 145), which could have been part, or even conceivably the initiation, of this adjustment of the chronology.

But whether or not this adjustment included Tom's visit—or Myrtle's party, for that matter—simply the movement forward of chapters 4 and 5, apparently after more than half the manuscript version was written, demonstrates clearly that Fitzgerald was working out the chronology of his story as he wrote and that he did not plot it beforehand. It is evident that at some time after composing the fifth chapter, he discovered that he had used either too little of his calendar for the narrative or too much of his narrative for the calendar.

The first of these emphases is, I think, much less likely, for it would seem to require that Fitzgerald's intention to end the main action with Gatsby's death at the end of the summer developed only after he had written well into his manuscript. But the clear implications in the first chapter—in manuscript as in published text—that the summer is the integral time frame of the story, and the subtler hints that Gatsby's story ends tragically, both argue against the implication. It seems safe to assume that, from the beginning, Fitzgerald intended to kill off Gatsby as the summer ended.

The opposite emphasis quite probably expresses the actual situation: Fitzgerald told Edmund Wilson that the "worst fault" in his novel was that he had given "no account (and had no feeling about or knowledge of) the emotional relations between Gatsby and Daisy from the time of their reunion to the catastrophe."[30] If this in fact means that, during the course of composition, he found himself unable to fictionalize those relations properly, it would seem that he discovered only around the middle of his manuscript that he had relatively little story left to tell, and therefore adjusted the calendar references to bring himself closer to the predetermined chronological end. According to the manuscript dating, the first five chapters are the events of only about the first third of the summer, up to the July third reunion and accounting for a bit less than a month's time. From the typescript version on, however, the same events are made to last until very late July, about twice the amount of time.

In effect, this is to suggest that the relative brevity of the novel was not completely foreseen by its author until well into composition. If the manuscript's indication of only a month's passage during the first five chapters can be taken as an index, Fitzgerald may have had the general expectation of writing a book almost twice as long as the final version of *Gatsby*.

Such a hypothesis might well explain something of the potentially digressive character of Myrtle's party, which (as has been suggested) might be more suitable for a more discursive narrative. It might also explain something of Fitzgerald's rather frequent and rather defensive comments on the length of *Gatsby*. Around 25 August 1924, he wrote to Perkins that the novel "runs only to about 50,000 words & I hope you won't shy at it," and, on 27 October 1924, that "The book is only a little over fifty thousand words long but . . . I'm anxious to charge two dollars for it and have it a *full size book*."[31] When sales were disappointing, Perkins noted the booksellers' skepticism about its length, but tactfully insisted that "the book is as full as it would have been if written to much greater length by another method" as if Fitzgerald needed such reassurance.[32] Fitzgerald was obviously stung when H. L. Mencken, a former idol, called *Gatsby* "a glorified anecdote," and he replied with the egregious bit of special pleading that if *Gatsby* was an anecdote, so was *The Brothers Karamazov*.[33] And in his introduction to the Modern Library edition of *Gatsby*, Fitzgerald claimed that "what I cut out of it both physically and emotionally would make another novel!"[34]—which on the evidence of the surviving drafts is not even a pardonable exaggeration. Some part of this testimony was merely apprehension, and then resentment, about the novel's sales. Still the relative brevity of *Gatsby* seems to have been a sensitive point with Fitzgerald, and perhaps in part because the brevity was not fully anticipated.[35]

There is one last minor matter to be dealt with in chapter 5: it has to do with Nick's employment. He is at home apparently all day when the reunion occurs: he goes into West Egg Village at 11:00 A.M. and, somewhat earlier, saw Klipspringer "wandering hungrily around the beach that morning" (p. 60). Yet the narrative refers to homeward-bound commuter trains that evening (p. 63), thus insisting it is a weekday. This leads to the reflection that, in spite of Nick's buying "a dozen volumes on banking and credit and investment securities" (p. 3) and regularly studying "a conscientious hour" (p. 38) in the library of the Yale Club, he often seems cavalier about working hours.

After the Sunday at Myrtle's, he is "half asleep in the cold lower level of Pennsylvania Station . . . waiting for the four o'clock train" (p. 25). Evidently, he is taking a Monday off.[36] "At nine o'clock" of the day of the lunch with Wolfsheim, he has not left for work when Gatsby drives up; and, although he can hardly arrive before ten,[37] he leaves early enough to keep the lunch date in a Forty-Second Street restaurant at noon (p. 54). On the day of the Plaza scene, he has left work early enough to hear the noon whistles on Queens side of the East River as he returns to

Long Island (p. 75). On the day of Gatsby's death, he finishes breakfast at 9:00; states shortly after, "Twelve minutes to my train," as if he regularly took the 9:15; misses "that train, and then another" (p. 120); falls asleep at his desk; and catches the 3:50 home. There is no direct statement that he leaves work early for his apparently frequent teas with Jordan, but they are continually said to be in the "afternoon" (pp. 44, 49, 104), and the tea he hosts is at 4:00 (p. 56). The reader cannot be sure, but Nick's employer might well have been suspicious.

This concern is not merely facetious. Perhaps Fitzgerald presumed a context in which a Yale man learning the bond business arrived around ten and left when he chose, but the matter appears analogous to Nick's seemingly callous affair with the girl from Jersey City, which is harder to justify. In both cases, I expect Fitzgerald merely overlooked what unflattering inferences might be drawn. When the narrative requires Nick to be somewhere other than at work, he will be there; when his Jersey City affair can provide some contrast with, or even delay before, his romance with Jordan, he will have it. These random details are rather like many of the time references: they are of some local significance in the progress of the narrative, but too little concern is given to whether they contradict other details or whether they constitute completely coherent patterns.

In the matter of Nick's employment, incidentally, the manuscript is less casual than the final text. The Warwick section originally had rather more detail on Nick at work, including his conclusion that "if you were competent and likeable, they [his superiors] were polite and receptive and kind" (MS, pp. 120–21); and in one of the draft sequences in the confrontation chapter, Nick's early return is explained by the day's being "a half holiday" (MS, p. 178). But Nick as wage earner, like Jordan as celebrity, is much weakened in revision, and a small strand of the story's verisimilitude is weakened as a result.

Chapter 6 (Gatsby's Second Party)

The chronology of chapter 6 is the most contradictory in the novel, and the process of composition that underlies it extremely complicated. In large part, the contradictions derive from revision, and especially from the relocation in this chapter of materials bearing on Gatsby's past that originally were narrated in later chapters. To compound the difficulties, these relocations have adversely affected the chronology of chapter 7 as well.

The task of investigation will be somewhat facilitated by thinking of chapter 6 as five consecutive sections, three dealing with summer events, and two with Gatsby's past: (1) the visit by the reporter that opens the chapter; (2) the account of Gatsby's years with Dan Cody; (3) the visit of Tom and his friends to Gatsby's; (4) the party at Gatsby's which Tom and Daisy attend; and (5) the lyrical closing paragraphs on Gatsby's incarnating his aspirations in Daisy. Of these sections, three—the reporter's visit, the Dan Cody material, and the incarnation passage—were all added to this chapter during galley revision.

The chapter opens with the placement of the reporter's visit "about this time" (p. 64), which should refer to the time of the last narrated incident—the reunion in very late July. In its present position, the reporter's interest seems to mark a stage in the growth of Gatsby's notoriety, beginning as early as Jordan's "You must know Gatsby" (p. 8) in chapter 1, and culminating with the opening of chapter 7, as the parties cease "when curiosity about Gatsby was at its highest" (p. 74). In fact, in both the manuscript and typescript versions, the reporter's visit and the ending of the parties were parts of the same opening section for chapter 7, and it was not until he revised the galleys that Fitzgerald split off the reporter section and used it to open chapter 6.[38] The new location causes no problem for the summer time scheme; the narrative has simply moved a small step forward in time from the reunion, with no necessary implication for the location of any other event.

The second section of the chapter is Nick's account of Gatsby's years with Dan Cody, the substance of which is relevant not to the time frame of the summer, but to that of Gatsby's past. Nick concludes the account with "He told me all this very much later" (p. 67); in fact, Gatsby tells him during their early morning talk on the day of the murder, at the very end of August. Thus, "very much later" works out, reasonably enough, to mean just about a month. Since Nick explicitly states that he has left his sequential narration of the events of the summer, again there is no problem for that time frame. Again, we are dealing with material that was relocated during the revision of the galleys; in the earlier versions the Dan Cody section was narrated at the time Nick learned it—that is, it was part of the large block of past history that Gatsby relates to Nick in chapter 8 on the morning before his murder (MS, pp. 218–20). As is well known, Perkins' letter of

20 November 1924 commented on this block of narrative, and Fitzgerald took the comment as advice to split the block apart.[39]

Thus, although the new opening of the chapter with the reporter's visit and the Dan Cody story accounted for little if any elapsing of the summer, each created an impression that has some temporal dimension. In combination, they also effect a distinct pause in the pacing of the summer narration; as Nick says after the Cody section, "So I take advantage of this short halt, while Gatsby, so to speak, caught his breath, to clear this set of misconceptions away" (p. 67). The "short halt" is entirely appropriate to the lessened intensity of the plot between Gatsby's ostensible attainment of his dream and the beginning of the counteractions that will destroy both it and him. And the topic of Gatsby's notoriety proposed by the reporter's curiosity affords a smooth and cogent transition to the genuine detail of his years with Cody.

All of these are significant effects achieved by the new opening, without in themselves creating difficulties for the summer time scheme. The integration of the new opening with the rest of the chapter is quite another matter and will be explored shortly. First, however, it will be convenient to deal with the incarnation passage that closes chapter 6. Like the reporter's visit and the Dan Cody story, this, too, is a relocation in the galley revision of material that occurs elsewhere in manuscript and typescript. In this case, the earlier versions place the incarnation in the confrontation chapter, chapter 7 of the novel, and have Gatsby (in effect) tell it to Nick between the time his parties cease and the day of the Plaza scene. Both the original and the final versions are of extreme interest in terms of Nick's function as narrator, but locating the discussion that evokes his lyrical extrapolation on the evening of Gatsby's second party again makes no problem for the chronology.

However, the dating of the two major events of chapter 6— Tom's visit and Gatsby's second party—is beset with contradiction. We have three direct temporal statements about the events: Tom and his friends visit Gatsby's "one Sunday afternoon" (p. 67); they ride off "under the August foliage" (p. 69); and the party takes place "on the following Saturday night" (p. 69).

More significant, however, are the three relative references to these events, which work out to be mutually contradictory. On the day of the visit to Gatsby's, Nick states, "For several weeks I didn't see him or hear his voice on the phone" (p. 67); thus, it is "several weeks" since Gatsby's reunion with Daisy.[40] Yet, within a page of Nick's "several weeks," Gatsby reminds Tom that they met "about two weeks ago," and Tom agrees, "That's right" (p. 68). Thus, it is "about two weeks" since the lunch with Wolfsheim, which itself occurred two days before the reunion.[41] The narrative requires that Nick's "several weeks" plus two days equal Gatsby's "about two weeks."

Further, at Gatsby's party six days later—"on the following Saturday night"—Nick, infected by Daisy's disappointment, reflects, "I'd enjoyed these same people only two weeks ago" (p. 70). But if Nick has not seen Gatsby since the reunion, his last previous opportunity to enjoy Gatsby's guests must have been some days earlier than the reunion. As a matter of fact, his last previous party must also have been earlier than the lunch with Wolfsheim, which is itself two days before than the reunion. There is no room for a party between the lunch and the reunion because all three days in the sequence are weekdays: on the day of the lunch, Gatsby drives Nick to work; on the following day, Nick "called up Daisy from the office" (p. 55); and on the evening of the reunion, he observes "electric trains, men-carrying, . . . plunging home" (p. 63).

The temporal contradictions have become positively Byzantine. For the narrative now insists that Nick's "only two weeks" that separate this party from his last party is equal to Gatsby's "about two weeks" (between the visit and the lunch with Wolfsheim) plus six days (between the visit on Sunday and the party on the following Saturday) plus some further number of days (between Nick's last previous party and the lunch with Wolfsheim). Equally, and even more impossibly, the narrative insists that Nick's "only two weeks" between his parties at Gatsby's is equal to his own "several weeks" (between the reunion and the visit) plus six days (between the visit and the party) plus two days (between the reunion and the lunch) plus some further number of days (between the lunch and Nick's last party when he enjoyed these same people). Resort to graphic display seems essential (see table).

As the display makes clear, the text has posited that the time between the first and the fifth of the events (AE) is virtually equivalent to the time between the second and the fourth (BD),[42] and, even more remarkably, that the time between the third and fourth (CD) is greater than either. Fitzgerald often uses the word *several* quite loosely, but he cannot have intended the "several weeks" between the reunion and Tom's visit to mean considerably less than two.

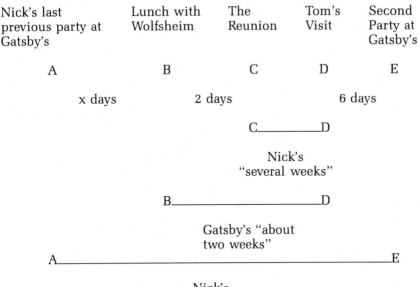

It must, I suppose, be allowed as literally possible for Nick to have attended a party at Gatsby's without seeing his host. Such a situation makes no sense in terms of their growing intimacy, and it would seem unusual enough to warrant mention in the narrative. But even if so unlikely a presumption were the case, it would merely reduce the three mutual contradictions to two, and, therefore, it is simply not credible that Fitzgerald intended any such solution.

The contradictions are somewhat the more surprising because the time references are relatively coherent in Fitzgerald's earlier versions of chapter 6. In manuscript, the chapter opens not with the reporter and the Dan Cody story, but with Tom's visit; it is located by the opening words of the chapter, "A few days after this" (MS, p. 143)—that is, a few days after the reunion, the last narrated event. And on the same manuscript page occurs Gatsby's recollection (which survives in the final text) of meeting Tom at the lunch with Wolfsheim "about two weeks ago." There is an imprecision here: if Tom's visit is only "a few days" after the reunion and the reunion two days after the lunch, Gatsby should recall meeting Tom about a week ago. For Fitzgerald *few*, like *several,* is quite a vague word; still, the manuscript posits no contradiction of the order of the final text.

As has already been noted, when Tom and his friends leave, Fitzgerald revised the manuscript to have them ride off "under the August foliage" (MS, p. 145), which also survives in the final text. The visit "a few days" after the reunion would take us to the very first days of August; Gatsby's "about two weeks" after the luncheon would take us perhaps a week into the month. The second might be a bit preferable, for, at Gatsby's second party—which, in the manuscript as in the final text, is on the Saturday following the Sunday of Tom's visit—Nick has the following reflection: "But I tried to imagine how this scene must appear to Daisy, how it had appeared to me on that June night two months before" (MS, p. 151). Since Nick's first party at Gatsby's was in mid-June, it is now apparently mid-August, and the events of the chapter have been dated with at least fair coherence.

All of the time references were retained in the typescript version, but in galley proof, Fitzgerald revised the first and last of these references—Tom's visit "a few days" after the reunion and Nick's recollection of his first party "two months before"—and thus created the contradictions of the published text. The reasons for these two revisions can be traced quite confidently; but they are completely different.

The first is the more complicated matter, although in general it seems that relocating Tom's visit in time derived from relocating it in narrative order, that is, by opening the chapter with the reporter's call and the Dan Cody material. The valuable effects attained by the new opening have already been noted, and it is well to recall that they required the elapsing of virtually no part of the summer. They did, however, create a significant pause in the pace of the narration, but they did so less by expending part of the summer, than by leaving it. There may well be an impression of time having passed, but, in fact, the narration rather clearly indicates it is dealing in the suspension, not the elapsing, of time when it speaks of the "short halt, while Gatsby, so to speak, caught his breath" (p. 67).

Immediately following, however, we pass from narrative impression to chronological documentation, as Fitzgerald provides a graceful transition for Nick and relocates Tom's visit: "It was a halt, too, in my association with his affairs. For several weeks I didn't see him or hear his voice on the phone" (p. 67). At the same time, he retained from the earlier version Gatsby's remembrance of meeting Tom "about two weeks ago" (p. 68), and thus produced the contradiction.

To make the matter even more fascinating—and more complicated—Nick's "several weeks" was in fact an afterthought during the galley revision. The original statement in galley revision was "For almost two weeks I didn't see him," which would, of course, have correlated with Tom and Gatsby's remembrance of meeting "about two weeks ago." But, later in galley revision, Fitzgerald crossed out the "almost two" in the typed copy, and wrote in "several"[43]—the contradictory reading of the final text.

The change in the galley revision from "almost two" to "several" admits of two explanations. First, Fitzgerald may have felt the need to lengthen the interval since the events of the last chapter. This, in turn, would mean that the sense of narrative pause that he created with the relocation of the reporter's visit and the Dan Cody story deceived him into documenting an actual and contradictory time lapse. (It might, of course, be argued that the greater time lapse was purposeful and that the error was Fitzgerald's forgetting to revise Gatsby's contradictory "about two weeks ago," which belonged to a rejected time-scheme.) The other possibility is that, in the galley revision, Fitzgerald went from "almost two weeks" to "several weeks" not because "several" was greater, but because it was more indeterminate, and thus because he was simply unsure about what he had committed himself to in terms of chronology. Ultimately, it is impossible to judge how sure he was about a mistaken time reference, but, clearly, he bungled the temporal link from his new opening to the materials he retained from the earlier versions.

The revision of the last of the manuscript's time references—Nick's recalling his first party "two months before" (MS, p. 151)—also contributed to the chronological incoherence of the final text, but the error derived from a totally different concern. The reference was replaced, again during galley revision, by Nick's "I'd enjoyed these same people only two weeks before. But what had amused me then turned septic on the air now" (p. 70).

The moment, it will be noted, has been revised from Nick's attempt to empathize with Daisy's feelings: "But I tried to imagine how this scene must appear to Daisy," which had utilized Nick's past experience, and hence the time reference, to aid in the attempt: "how it had appeared to me on that June night two months before" (MS, p. 151). In the final version Nick participates totally in Daisy's revulsion: the party has "turned septic" for him; and the time reference becomes an index to Nick's surprise at the reversal of his own feelings. From this second point of view, the briefer the time since his enjoyment, the more striking his current distaste. Accordingly, Fitzgerald wrote "only two weeks before," which sharpens the reversal of attitude nicely, but makes nonsense of the chronology.

Perhaps he had the sense that "two weeks" would put Nick's experience back safely before Tom's visit six days before. In any case, the revision may serve as an instructively typical case of the relatively small awareness Fitzgerald seems always to have had about exactly when his events took place and of the relatively low priority temporal coherence had in comparison to local narrative effect. The extremely small focus of much of Fitzgerald's revision has been widely praised for its sharpening and heightening of his style, but demonstrably, it could have unfortunate effects as well.

Although the revision of chapter 6 badly muddled the chronology of the events, which had been placed with reasonable coherence in the earlier versions, it would of course be foolish to claim the revision was not in general quite successful. As has been indicated, the new placement of the reporter's visit creates a miniature process of the growth of Gatsby's notoriety, and the relocation of the Dan Cody material provides a major step in the gradual unravelling of Gatsby's mystery. Further, the later version of the party is a huge improvement over that of the manuscript, which stresses the evening's rather silly rustic motif; in terms of theme and character, the conversation about repeating the past is extremely well considered; and the new closing with the incarnation passage is wonderfully poignant and resonant.

Yet none of these achievements was attained by chronological contradiction; indeed, almost nowhere in the novel can Fitzgerald's failures with his time scheme be justified as means to an artistic end. They are simply narrative errors, and what is admirable in the novel would be equally as admirable had they been corrected. In fact, what is admirable may have been somewhat more admirable for having been set in a more convincing and less distracting fictional world.

Chapter 7 (The Confrontation)

Chapter 7, in the largest part, deals with the events of a single day—that of the confrontation between Tom and Gatsby at the

Plaza, which itself presents chronological problems. But before the narrative reaches that critical day, it establishes a three-day time sequence which also requires investigation.

The chapter opens with the ending of Gatsby's parties: "It was when curiosity about Gatsby was at its highest that the lights in his house failed to go on one Saturday night—and, as obscurely as it began, his career as Trimalchio was over" (p. 74). Nick goes over on that evening and leaves a message with the villainous-looking new butler; "Next day"—therefore, by extrapolation, Sunday—Gatsby phones and relays Daisy's invitation "to lunch at her house to-morrow" (p. 75)—therefore, again extrapolating, Monday. The day of the lunch at the Buchanans' is also the day of the confrontation at the Plaza and of Myrtle's death; the following day—by a final extrapolation, Tuesday—will be the day of Gatsby's murder. It is necessary to call attention to the extrapolation process, for, after the Saturday when the parties end, the text will not specify the day of the week again. Although these locations of particular events on particular days of the week are the unavoidable implications of the text, there is no reason to presume they were consciously present in Fitzgerald's imagination and, as will be seen, some indication later that he was unaware of them.

The day of the confrontation is characterized as "almost the last, certainly the warmest of summer" (p. 75), which, according to Fitzgerald's ordinary usage, the impression of most readers, and the evidence of the drafts, should be 30 August. The implication is borne out by the heavy use of nature symbolism in the next chapter, which portrays the day of Gatsby's death as either the last day of summer or the first of autumn or—perhaps the best interpretation—both. Thus, ideally his death should be dated 31 August or 1 September.

The extrapolated succession of days, among other things, demonstrates the irrelevance of the actual 1922 calendar to Fitzgerald's design. The last Saturday of August of 1922 was in fact the twenty-sixth—the night the parties end; the last Tuesday—the day Gatsby dies—was the twenty-ninth, a most unsatisfactory two or three days from what the symbolism requires.

There is also difficulty with the location of the beginning of the three-day sequence, that is, the night on which the parties end. Since it is a Saturday, like the night of Gatsby's second party, the two events are exactly one week or exactly two weeks apart; but, on the basis of the final text, there seems no reliable way to determine which, and, thus, no reliable way to know whether

Fitzgerald intended to place the action relatively close to or relatively distant from the preceding chapter.

Nick learns from his Finnish housekeeper that Gatsby has dismissed his servants, "a week ago" (p. 75) and has replaced them with a set of Wolfsheim's henchmen, who have in the meanwhile evoked the dislike and suspicion of the locals because they are reclusive, unbribeable, and messy. Since Nick is in possession of this information when Gatsby phones on Sunday, it seems that the Finn must tell him either on the Saturday evening the parties end or early the next day (although it would be odd, under the terms of her employment, that she be at Nick's either time).[44] Her gossip rather suggests that two weeks have passed since the party Nick, Tom, and Daisy attended, for literally her "week ago" cannot refer back both to the night of the party and to the dismissal of the servants that succeeded it. And if her "week ago" actually means a little less than seven days, there seems to be insufficient time for Gatsby to recruit and install his new staff and for them to alienate the village.

On the other hand, while talking to Gatsby on the phone, Nick reflects on his motives for ending the parties: "So the whole caravansary had fallen in like a card house at the disapproval in her eyes" (p. 75). This sounds as if Gatsby's reaction was characteristically immediate and extreme and as if he fired his servants on the morning after the party, as the "week ago" would require. It must also be allowed as distinctly strange to imagine that Gatsby gave another party a week after the one Daisy had attended, and *then* decided to end his career as host. Obviously, the narrative provides implications of a one-week interval since Gatsby's second party as well.

The evidence of the drafts is of no help in choosing between a one- or two-week interval. In the manuscript, Nick's calling at Gatsby's is preceded by "For two weeks I hadn't seen him" (MS, p. 159); the interval in the typescript version became "for several weeks" (Gal., 34); and in the revision of the galleys, it went from "for a week after the last party, where Daisy hadn't had a good time," to simply "for a week," and then was cut totally.[45]

To my mind, what stands in the final text, makes a lapse of just one week between the party and the lights' going out somewhat the more likely implication.[46] But one simply cannot have confidence in the implication when the final text itself is ambiguous and the evidence of the drafts is that Fitzgerald could not determine where to locate the opening of his chapter.

Mention of the draft versions of chapter 7 requires some discussion of the unusual state of the manuscript of what was the most troublesome and heavily revised chapter in the novel. Both the unrevised and the revised galleys differ substantially from the manuscript version, which is itself not a single draft of the narrative, but five sequences, the first four of which overlap and all of which contain at least some alternative detail. In a sense, this is a difference only in degree from the other eight chapters, which, although they can be read through as reasonably coherent portions of the narrative, in fact contain within them pages or paragraphs or sentences that have been salvaged and recopied from earlier stages of composition. However, the obtrusiveness of such material everywhere except in the seventh chapter merely causes some unevenness or an occasional minor contradiction. The five sequences in chapter 7 are so strongly alternative to, and sometimes mutually exclusive of, one another that the manuscript here is clearly a collection of elements from different stages of composition, which have not been even provisionally integrated.

Of the five sequences, the first two, A and B, are relevant to the time period from the end of the parties to the confrontation, which became three days in the final text. In sequence A (as in all subsequent stages of composition), the parties end on a Saturday; then Gatsby returns Nick's visit "several evenings later" and invites him to "lunch at Daisy's house next Saturday" (MS, p. 160). Gatsby's visit to Nick's "several evenings" after the parties end survived in the typescript version, but the lunch at Daisy's "next Saturday"—which would have put the confrontation exactly a week after the parties end[47]—was replaced in the typescript by some alternative detail from the overlapping sequence B: "The thirtieth of August was a half holiday and I had promised Tom Buchanan to lunch with them at East Egg. . . . It was a broiling day, almost the last and certainly the hottest of the summer" (MS, p. 178).[48]

Thus, in the typescript version, there is no narrative connection between Gatsby's visit to Nick and the invitation to lunch at the Buchanans', and no suggestion about their relation in time. In galley revision, however, Fitzgerald restored the invitation and shrank the period between the end of the parties and the confrontation to three days, very probably to reflect a shrinkage in content.

During Gatsby's visit to Nick's in manuscript sequence A, he tells Nick of his romance in Louisville, including a version of the passage on his incarnating his aspirations in Daisy, does a good deal of maudlin expatiation on his current troubles, and even sings a notably soppy song of his own composition.[49] With a good many minor changes, everything but the song reappeared in the typescript version. In galley revision, however, the incarnation passage was transferred to the closing of chapter 6, together with something of Nick's reaction to Gatsby's "appalling sentimentality" (p. 74)—which in manuscript had been provoked by the song. The balance of Gatsby's lachrymose complaints were simply, and wisely, junked; as a result, his visit "several evenings later" (MS, p. 160) had virtually no content left, and became a phone call "next day" (p. 75).

I would suggest that the lessening in content and the lessening in time went hand in hand. The situation here looks opposite to, but analogous with, Fitzgerald's final revision of the opening of chapter 6. There, the addition of the reporter's call and the Dan Cody story created the impression of an increase in elapsed time, and the impression was endorsed by adding a contradictory time reference—"several weeks." Here, the removal of the incarnation passage and Gatsby's lamentation seemed to bring events closer, and, concurrently, the time lapse was contracted from "several evenings" to "next day" (and the event itself degraded from a visit to a phone call). In both cases, it seems that the alteration of narrative effect dictated an alteration in chronology.

The specification of the day of the confrontation as "the thirtieth of August," in both manuscript (MS, p. 178) and typescript (Gal., 35), disappeared in galley revision, although the temporal location seems always to have remained the same in Fitzgerald's imagination. Throughout the composition of *Gatsby*, he very seldom dated any of the events of the summer precisely; the manuscript's location of the reunion on July third (MS, p. 125) is, in fact, the only other instance. Yet the specificity of the timetable's "July 5, 1922" (p. 40), and of the self-improvement schedule's "September 12, 1906" (p. 116)[50] gives rise to the suspicion that he was especially wary of committing himself to exact dates that would have to correlate within the limited time frame of the summer.

It is needless to say at this point that Fitzgerald's progressive revisions of this portion of the novel make investigating its chronology extraordinarily complicated. It seems in order, therefore, to summarize in tabular form the development of the temporal placement of the narrative events from the reporter's visit at the beginning of chapter 6 up to the day of the confrontation in chapter 7. (See table, p. 69.) The events comprise a natural grouping, not just

                                    July

A. Lunch with Wolfsheim--"late in July"
B. The reunion--two days later

                                   August

Manuscript/Typescript   Revised Galleys/Final Text

Chapter 6

                                         1. Reporter's visit
                                                "about this time" (viz.
                                                   the reunion)
                                             [The Dan Cody story--from
                                                MS chapter 8]

1. Tom's visit   2. Tom's visit
        "Sunday"   "Sunday"
        "a few days" after reunion   "several weeks" after reunion
                                                ("about two weeks" after
                                                   reunion canceled in RG)
        "about two weeks" after   "about two weeks" after
           lunch with Wolfsheim   lunch with Wolfsheim

2. Gatsby's second party   3. Gatsby's second party
        "following Saturday" after   "following Saturday" after
           Tom's visit   Tom's visit
        "two months" after Nick's   "two weeks" after Nick's
           first party at Gatsby's   last party at Gatsby's
                                             [The incarnation passage]

Chapter 7

3. Reporter's visit
        "about this time" (Gatsby's
           second party?)

4. End of parties   4. End of parties
        "Saturday"   "Saturday"
        MS: "two weeks" after   RG: "a week" after
           Gatsby's second party   Gatsby's second party
        TS: "several weeks" after   Final: no specification
           Gatsby's second party

5. Gatsby's visit   5. Gatsby's phone call
        "several evenings" after   "next day" after end of
           end of parties   parties
        [The incarnation passage]

6. Confrontation   6. Confrontation
        ("next Saturday" after
           Gatsby's visit only in
           MS sequence A)
        "thirtieth of August . . .   "almost the last" day of
           almost the last" day of   summer
           summer

because they occur in the most heavily revised sections of the novel, but because they are in the published text, and seem always to have been in the earlier drafts, the events of August 1922.[51]

These materials not only indicate a good deal about how the chronology of this portion of the novel evolved, they also suggest some general conclusions about Fitzgerald's temporal concerns in *Gatsby*. There seems never to have been compete clarity about the interrelation of the events of August 1922, although there seems never to have been complete chaos either. For example, that the confrontation and the murder occur, in effect, on the last two days of summer, appears always to have been firm in Fitzgerald's mind. With these incidents establishing the further limit, there seems also to have been the intention to fit the five preceding incidents within the calendar month, and at only one point in composition did Fitzgerald's datings threaten to exceed that limit.

It is also evident that, in his final revision, Fitzgerald introduced two temporal effects that were not present in the earlier versions of *Gatsby*: time elapses at the beginning of chapter 6 before the major event of Tom's visit; and time is compressed at the beginning of chapter 7 before the major event of the confrontation. In both cases, the addition or deletion of materials seems to have been of more significance than the alteration of the time references. The addition of the reporter's visit and the Dan Cody material to open chapter 6 resulted in an increased time lapse and marked the pause in Gatsby's affairs after the reunion more strongly; the deletion of the reporter's visit and most of the content of Gatsby's visit to Nick toward the beginning of chapter 7 resulted in a decrease and moved more quickly from the ending of the parties to the climactic confrontation. It may well have been that achieving these temporal impressions was of lesser concern than finding more effective locations for the materials relating to Gatsby's past, but even if these impressions were, so to speak, by-products, still they are themselves of some value.

In each case, however, the new temporal indicator that was provided—the "several weeks" between the reunion and Tom's visit, the implicit three-day sequence from the end of the parties to the confrontation—resulted in incoherence. That very incoherence suggests that the indicators were dictated by the temporal impressions which the alterations in content created, and thus that the temporal impressions were of greater concern to Fitzgerald than the chronological specifications.

But speaking of the narrative of *Gatsby* in terms of impressions or inner dynamics in no way resolves problems of chronology. Verisimilitude demands that these concerns be translated into a coherent time scheme, and it is at this level that Fitzgerald continually errs. If these tabulated materials suggest that his revision attained some desirable narrative effects, they also demonstrate much that is less than laudable.

If, for example, the increase in elapsed time with the opening of chapter 6 purposefully moves Tom's visit forward in time and locates it "several weeks" after the reunion, then it was the merest of inadvertence not to cancel Gatsby's "two weeks ago," which belongs to an earlier, rejected time scheme. If time is compressed meaningfully to a three-day sequence from the end of the parties to the confrontation, then the implication of those three days remains significant for the final events of the novel. Finally, if one is disposed to see a coherent relationship between time expanded in chapter 6 before Tom's visit and time compressed in chapter 7 before the confrontation, it must also be remembered that between the two lies the time gap from the second party to the end of the parties—which is simply unclear in the final text, as it appears to have been in Fitzgerald's mind.

It should be noted that he seemed to have had quite serious difficulties with time references that crossed the boundaries of a chapter. The expiration of time here between the second party—the last event of chapter 6—and the end of the parties—the first event of chapter 7—went in draft from "two weeks" to "a week," and then, in the final text, was left unspecified and ambiguously suggesting both one week and two. Similarly, Fitzgerald produced contradiction by referring to Tom's visit in chapter 6 both as "several weeks" after the reunion in chapter 5 and as "two weeks" after the lunch with Wolfsheim in chapter 4. He used the individual chapters as compositional units in writing *Gatsby*, and this work method itself may well have influenced the novel's chronological weaknesses.

That the time period between Gatsby's second party and the end of the parties is unspecified and ambiguous is also evidence of a suspicion which has already been broached: that Fitzgerald's lack of temporal specification is sometimes wariness based on realization of his own uncertainty. The drafts continually change this time period, but they continually specify it. Yet Fitzgerald dropped this specification, of which he seems to have been most unsure, while adding in the same galley revision two or three other specifications that proved incoherent. His reticence about this particular interval looks like more than coincidence can account for.

The drafts' changes of specification for this period support another and related suspicion: that for Fitzgerald the word *several* is more an evasion than a specification. The period was "two weeks" in manuscript, increased to "several weeks" in the typescript, and then shrank all the way to "a week" in galley revision, before finally being dropped. Yet the typescript's "several weeks" correlates with nothing else at any stage of composition; in fact, if "several" is taken to mean three or more (as it means in chapter 3, p. 37), it is the single time reference in all the versions that would have expanded the time between Tom's visit and the confrontation beyond the month of August. It seems very likely that what Fitzgerald ultimately meant by the typescript's "several weeks" was "I don't know how long, but I'll get back to it later."

Mention should also be made here of the revision of Nick's remembering his earlier experience at Gatsby's from "two months ago" to "two weeks ago." As has been explained, this is a special case, not an adjustment to the relocation of materials, but merely a heightening of Nick's momentary feeling of revulsion. But pursuing this local effect by a time reference created the narrative demand that it correlate with other time references, a demand Fitzgerald failed to fulfill.

Finally, these materials demonstrate firmly that Fitzgerald was by no means totally unconcerned with his novel's chronology. It was not a matter of highest priority, obviously, and considerations such as temporal impression or narrative pace were certainly more important to him. But nothing makes sense of this record of his changing, adding, and canceling time references but that he was making efforts toward producing a coherent chronology. None too successful efforts, but efforts nevertheless.

All of these temporal problems relate to the narrative prior to the single day on which the bulk of the action of chapter 7 occurs—the day of the confrontation. This day presents three more chronological difficulties.

The first occurs when Tom stops at the gas station on the way to New York, and Wilson confides, "I just got wised up to something funny the last two days" (p. 82). The "something funny" is, of course, Myrtle's infidelity, and, since it is now (by extrapolation) Monday, Wilson is claiming he "got wised up" on the preceding Saturday. He further explains, "that's why I been bothering you about the car" (p. 82); he had phoned Tom just as

Nick and Gatsby arrived, presumably about 12:30 since Nick heard the noon whistles in Long Island City (p. 75) as he returned for the luncheon. In chapter 8, however, Wilson tells Michaelis that his suspicions were aroused by the dogleash in Myrtle's drawer: "I found it yesterday afternoon. She tried to tell me about it, but I knew it was something funny" (p. 106). Since by this time, it is after "three o'clock" (p. 105) on Tuesday morning, the day of Gatsby's death, Wilson is claiming to have found the leash not only two days after he "got wised up," according to his statement to Tom, but even a short time after he phoned Tom about the car.[52]

The last two chronological problems in chapter 7 pertain to smaller time frames, and almost surely are interrelated. The first concerns the management of time during the Plaza scene. The group arrives, we are told, at "four o'clock" (p. 84), and for the next six pages of text, we have virtually continuous dialogue. This is by far the most extended dialogue scene in the novel, with no indication that more than a couple of minutes at most elapse between any exchange. Much the longest interruption is the arrival of the waiter, which could presumably require three or four minutes. But the arrival interrupts Tom's challenge of Gatsby's attendance at Oxford, and, after the waiter leaves, the topic is immediately resumed: "'I told you I went there,' said Gatsby" (p. 86). Even the longest interruption of the dialogue is extremely brief.

The scene culminates with Tom's accusations about Gatsby's activities, after which Gatsby "began to talk excitedly to Daisy, denying everything, defending his name against accusations that had not been made ... as the afternoon slipped away" (p. 90). Very shortly after, Gatsby and Daisy leave, and, "after a moment" (p. 90), Tom, Nick, and Jordan prepare to go. As Nick reports, "It was seven o'clock when we got into the coupé" (p. 91).

Three hours on the clock have elapsed since the arrival at the Plaza, yet because of the extreme sense of immediacy the dialogue creates, our impression is that the scene—at least up to Gatsby's self-justification—utilizes very little more time than it takes to read. And however long Gatsby's rebuttal is, it would be grotesque to imagine that it goes on for the two hours or more that seem necessary for the afternoon to slip away. The problem here is not a contradiction; it is a failure of effect. And the failure is surprising, since Fitzgerald managed a convincing sense of clock time elapsing many other places in Gatsby. If one compares

Nick's first party at Gatsby's or Wilson's tortured night after the accident or—the novel's outstanding success in this regard—the drunken, dislocated hours of the Sunday at Myrtle's, it becomes quite evident that, in the Plaza scene, Fitzgerald is requiring time to pass without creating adequate narrative detail to account for its passage.

Fitzgerald himself may have been aware of this failure. His feeling that, in spite of repeated rewriting, he never quite got the Plaza scene right has often been cited; and on 10 April 1925—the very day *Gatsby* was published—he wrote Perkins, calling the scene "hurried and ineffective,"[53] just the effect that the incoherence between perceived time and narrative time creates.

Fitzgerald's revision of the scene was fairly clearly at the heart of the problem, but, since the same revision seems also to have influenced the last of chapter 7's chronological inconsistencies, it will be more convenient to discuss the revision after presenting the problem of the time frame of Myrtle's death and Tom's return to East Egg.

By Michaelis's testimony, Myrtle is killed at perhaps 7:10: at "a little after seven" (p. 91), he hears her screaming at Wilson, and "a moment later she rushed out into the dusk" (p. 92), to be struck by the car. This suits well enough with Gatsby and Daisy's departure from the Plaza a little before seven, and the statement of the "pale well-dressed negro" that Daisy was speeding, "Going fifty, sixty" (p. 94).

Tom, Nick, and Jordan stop at the garage very shortly after the accident, and, after Tom has impressed on Wilson that it was not he who killed Myrtle, they leave, passing "a hurried doctor, case in hand, who had been sent for in wild hope half an hour ago" (p. 95). Thus, it is approximately 7:45.

Yet when the three arrive at the Buchanans', as Jordan announces, "It's only half-past nine" (p. 95). Now, the East Egg area, we are told in chapter 1, is "twenty miles from the city" (p. 3), and Wilson's garage, we are told in chapter 2, is "about half way between West Egg and New York" (p. 15); adding a couple of miles to Tom's estate at the very tip of East Egg, the trip is perhaps twelve miles. Thus, although "the coupé raced along through the night" (p. 95), and made no stops—Tom has forgotten to leave Nick in West Egg—the twelve-mile trip from the garage takes about an hour and three-quarters; the coupé raced along at almost seven miles an hour.

Evidently, Fitzgerald wanted it to be late enough for Nick to discover, and leave, Gatsby in the dark outside Daisy's house, "watching over nothing" (p. 98). Even more documentably than with the Plaza scene, however, he has neglected to provide narrative incident to allow the necessary time to elapse that would justify the symbolic picture.

The temporal incoherences in both the Plaza scene and the trip from the garage derive in large part from Fitzgerald's revisions. In the relevant portion of the manuscript, there is no time indicated for the arrival at the Plaza, and the departure occurs later: "It was eight o'clock by my watch when we got into the coupe" (MS, p. 200).[54] But the manuscript accounts for the lapse of time somewhat better by supplying a fair amount of physical activity: as the wedding music floats up, "Hilariously we danced, Daisy and I, Gatsby and Jordan, while Tom at the telephone watched us with unrestful eyes"; and after Daisy appeals to Nick and Jordan to persuade Tom, who is drinking, to leave, "I tried and so did Jordan" (MS, p. 193). In the typescript version, the departure is moved back to "seven o'clock" (Gal., 42), and the physical action is retained and in part expanded by adding to Nick's and Jordan's attempts to make Tom leave: "We tried intermittently for an hour" (Gal., 40).[55] The galley revisions, however, cut the hilarious dancing and the appeals to Tom while retaining the departure at seven o'clock. It was an especially unfortunate change. For it not only left the confrontation scene without the sort of activity that would have created the sense of time elapsing that is lacking in the final text; it also retained the earlier departure, which put the cast on the road earlier and aggravated the problem of Tom's arriving home at 9:30.

Unlike the Plaza scene, the portion of the chapter dealing with Myrtle's death and the return to East Egg was not heavily revised. The sending for the doctor "half an hour ago" (MS, p. 209) and the 9:30 arrival at Tom's (MS, p. 210), for example, are in the manuscript version; and thus most of the incoherence concerning the trip from the garage was present from the beginning. The manuscript, however, has Michaelis, coming outside at "about half past seven," and Myrtle shouting and running into the road "a moment later" (MS, p. 203). But the typescript version revised this to "a little after seven" (Gal., 42)—the reading of the final text—undoubtedly to correspond to its movement of the departure from the Plaza to 7:00. Thus, the inconsistency of Tom's return home becomes graver for having more time to account for.

Chapter 8 (The Murder)

The first matter to be dealt with in chapter 8 is the establishment of Gatsby's death on almost exactly the last day of the summer, 31 August. This seems to have been the dating most firmly set in Fitzgerald's imagination, not just because this is the day after "almost the last" day of summer (and August thirtieth in the drafts), but also because of the symbolic ambience of the scene.

In *Gatsby*, times of the day and the year are usually at least atmospheric and frequently symbolic. One recalls immediately the darkness through which Gatsby yearns for the green light, Nick's wanderings in "the enchanted metropolitan twilight" (p. 38), and the nostalgic dark winter of his returns to the midwest "at Christmas time" (p. 117). In the incarnation passage there is something very like a generalized assertion of such symbolic meaning: "Now it was a cool night with that mysterious excitement in it which comes at the two changes of the year" (p. 74).

These two changes to and from the summer of 1922 bear the same significance. At the novel's opening, Nick says, "And so with the sunshine and the great bursts of leaves growing on the trees, just as things grow in fast movies, I had that familiar conviction that life was beginning over again with the summer" (p. 3). And Jordan—ironically, as it eventuates—in the stifling heat of the Plaza scene, asserts the symbolic power of the other change: "Life starts all over again when it gets crisp in the fall" (p. 78).

The change begins as the group drives home from the Plaza "through the cooling twilight" (p. 91). On the next day, the day of Gatsby's death, fall seems to arrive. It is "a cool, lovely day" (p. 101); "there was an autumn flavor in the air"; Gatsby's gardener warns, "Leaves'll start falling pretty soon" (p. 102); and, indeed, Gatsby goes down to his pool, "among the yellowing trees," and dies there, "the touch of a cluster of leaves" (p. 108) revolving around the mattress that bears his body.

Clearly, Fitzgerald wanted the summer, Gatsby's life, and, for that matter, Nick's youth and his illusions, all to end at the same time. To achieve this, he speeds up time—"just as things grow in fast movies"—so that the leaves yellow and fall, summer ends, and autumn arrives within a single day. He does so properly, I think, for, without the dislocation of realistic time, the sense that Gatsby, and romantic idealism, die as inevitably and poignantly as the summer could not have been achieved. Matching the effect to the calender is not quite possible, for, ideally, it should not only be 31 August, the last day of summer, but at least 1 September, the beginning of the fall, as well. Although the instance here may be thought of as a representative case of Fitzgerald's willingness to disrupt chronology for some local emotional or symbolic effect, it is, I believe, the only time in *Gatsby* where such disruption was necessitated by the effect.

Chapter 8 was significantly revised during composition, though by no means as extensively as chapters 6 and 7, and the revision affected the account of his life that Gatsby gives Nick far more than the events of his last day. As has been noted, the Dan Cody material was moved to the opening of chapter 6, and the truth of Gatsby's stay at Oxford was worked into the Plaza scene in chapter 7, but virtually all of the references to the change of the seasons were already present in the manuscript version. In fact, there was more, quite odd, such reference: while Wilson and Michaelis keep their vigil, "The September bugs were like blown sand around the dullish light" (MS, p. 229). "The September bugs" are, I take it, the bugs that are flying about on this, apparently first, September day; curiously enough, Fitzgerald's revision to the final text's "hard brown beetles" (p. 105) makes it clear that he was thinking of the insects known as June bugs.

The events of the day are generally quite coherent in time; there is even some successful coordination of the movements of three different characters. Nick is wakened "toward dawn" by the sound of a taxi at Gatsby's, goes over immediately, and meets Gatsby, who says he waited at Daisy's until "about four o'clock" (p. 98). (Where he got a taxi at 4:00 A.M. is not revealed.) Gatsby then tells Nick of his life from his years with Dan Cody to his learning at Oxford of Daisy's engagement to Tom. They finish breakfast at nine; and Nick, after missing two trains, leaves for work, promising to phone at noon (p. 102). At the office, Nick receives a call from Jordan "just before noon" (p. 103) and, after trying unsuccessfully to call Gatsby, decides at "just noon" to take "the three-fifty train" (p. 108) back to West Egg.

Meanwhile, Wilson has set off on his odyssey of revenge. He begins at some unspecified time in the morning: we are told that the exhausted Michaelis cooked breakfast at "six o'clock," ate, went to bed, and "awoke four hours later" (p. 107) to find Wilson gone. Wilson reaches Gad's Hill at "noon" (p. 107) and, as we later learn, goes to Tom's to discover who drove the death car. In chapter 9, we are told that Tom and Daisy left "early that afternoon" (p. 109), and, at their final meeting, Tom confesses to Nick that Wilson arrived "while we were getting ready to leave" (p. 120). Wilson's arrival then can be placed about 1:00 or 1:30, for "by half-past two" (p. 107), he is in West Egg, asking the way to Gatsby's.

"At two o'clock" (p. 108), Gatsby goes to his pool, leaving instructions that he is to be notified in case of a phone call. His butler waits for the call "until four o'clock," which is "long after there was anyone to give it to if it came" (p. 108). Gatsby's death, therefore, should be about 3:00, in order to make sense of the "long after" and to give Wilson time to arrive from West Egg. The last incident of the chapter is Nick's arrival, "from the station directly to Gatsby's house" (p. 108), to discover the body, presumably a little before 5:00.

The general scheme is quite consistent, but anomalies persist here as elsewhere. Although it is not so much a chronological problem as a problem with a chronological dimension, the matter of the phone calls to Gatsby is badly bungled. Nick returns from work early because he cannot contact Gatsby by phone: "I called Gatsby's house a few minutes later, but the line was busy. I tried four times; finally an exasperated central told me the wire was being kept open for long distance from Detroit" (p. 104). This sounds like the suspicious calls Gatsby often receives, but, at this point in the narrative, it makes no sense.

Gatsby knows Nick plans to call at noon, because he promised to do so just before leaving for work:

> "I'll call you up," I said finally.
> "Do, old sport."
> "I'll call you about noon."
>
> (p. 102)

Even more important, Gatsby expects (or at least hopes for) a phone call from Daisy. Immediately after Nick promises to call, Gatsby says, "'I suppose Daisy'll call too.' He looked at me anxiously, as if he hoped I'd corroborate this" (p. 103). It is a call from Daisy, not from some confederate, that he tells the butler to wait for, as Nick's speculation makes clear: "I have an idea that Gatsby himself didn't believe it would come, and perhaps he no longer cared" (p. 108). But it makes no sense for him to expect the call, or to care about it or not, if "the wire was being kept open for long distance from Detroit." Evidently, Fitzgerald wanted Nick isolated, helpless and apprehensive, as the tragedy approaches. But he achieved the effect only at the cost of a narrative contradiction.[56]

There is also much that is troublesome in the materials connected with Wilson in this chapter. We are told that Michaelis, after "three o'clock" on the night he keeps vigil with Wilson, hears a car that "sounded to him like the car that hadn't stopped a few hours before" (p. 105). Since Myrtle was killed shortly after 7:00 P.M., Fitzgerald here has elasticized "a few" to mean about eight.

Almost immediately after, Wilson "blurted out that a couple of months ago his wife had come from the city with her face bruised and her nose swollen" (p. 105). The time reference, though quite colloquial, is in fact precise; it is now the last day of August, almost exactly two months from Myrtle's party in very early July, when Tom broke her nose. And the precision is achieved by revision, for the manuscript has "a month ago" (MS, p. 229).[57] However, the manuscript also specifies "her face all bruised and her nose broken," and reemphasizes the detail by having Wilson flinch "when he heard himself say the words bruised and broken" (MS, p. 229). But the final text gives Myrtle only a swollen nose, as if the more serious injury would have been too much to leave even Wilson without suspicion. Fitzgerald seems unwilling to pay the legitimate fictional price for the brilliant detail in chapter 2: "Making a short deft movement, Tom Buchanan broke her nose with his open hand" (p. 25).[58]

He is also quite careless two pages later, when Wilson sets out. We are told that he buys "a sandwich that he didn't eat, and a cup of coffee" in Gad's Hill at "noon"; and later in the same paragraph, he is reported in West Egg asking for Gatsby's house at "half-past two." In the middle of the same paragrapgh, however, we are told that between the two reported appearances, "for three hours he disappeared from view" (p. 107). Allowing Wilson a little time not to eat his sandwich results in his managing to disappear for "three hours" in about two hours and twenty minutes.[59]

Generally, Wilson's journey of vengeance seems impossibly long, an impression that stems in part from the widely known fact that in Fitzgerald's imagination, East Egg and West Egg are the fictional equivalents of Great Neck and Manhasset Neck, and the valley of ashes present-day Flushing Meadows. But formally,

it is not this landscape, but a fictional one, that Wilson tra-
verses,[60] and the episode is further removed from scrutiny by the
narrative's vagueness about when he starts. We are told only that
Michaelis made breakfast at "six o'clock," ate, slept for "four
hours" (p. 107), and found Wilson gone; he may have left any
time between perhaps 6:30 and 10:15.

Strictly in terms of what the narrative does say, however, it is
possible to deduce a great deal about the geography, the chronology, and the ultimate improbability of the journey. Wilson's journey may be thought of in four stages: from the garage to Gad's
Hill, from Gad's Hill to Tom's house, from Tom's to West Egg
Village, and thence to Gatsby's. It has already been calculated
that from the garage (halfway on the twenty miles from New York
to the Eggs) to Tom's house at the very tip of West Egg is about
twelve miles. From here, Wilson must walk perhaps two miles
back down the east shore of the courtesy bay—Nick says the eggs
are "enormous" (p. 3); then some distance along the south of the
bay—presume a mile; then up the western shore to West Egg
Village—presume another mile, for a total of about four. The
Village is, of course, not immediately adjacent to Gatsby's estate,
but on the day of the ride to New York, Nick speaks of it as
relatively close: "We hadn't reached West Egg Village before Gatsby began . . ." (p. 42)—presume one more mile. The entire journey seems to be something like seventeen miles, "on foot all the
time" (p. 107), and Wilson has had no food and no sleep the
night before. Since twenty-five miles is about as far as a man can
walk in a day, his feat verges on the astonishing.

In terms of time, Wilson covers the final mile of his journey
between 2:30, when he asks in the Village for Gatsby's, and 3:00
(or even a bit earlier), when, as has already been calculated, he
kills Gatsby. His trip around the bay is more difficult; it is about
four miles, and he has already walked twelve. It must take something more than an hour; thus, he must leave Tom's by about
1:15 to be in West Egg by 2:30. He must spend some time at
Tom's, however, for Tom claims that initially "I sent down word
that we weren't in," and then that "he tried to force his way
upstairs" (p. 120). Ten minutes at Tom's seems a minimum, and
this puts Wilson's arrival back to about 1:05.

Since we know that Wilson reached Gad's Hill at noon and
stopped to order food, we have something of a fix on that locale.
It is close enough to Tom's for Wilson to walk in an hour or a
bit less; thus, it is two or three miles away. By subtraction, Gad's
Hill, therefore, is nine or ten miles from the valley of ashes. The

narrative makes it sound quite otherwise: "He must have been tired and walking slowly, for he didn't reach Gad's Hill until noon" (p. 107). The natural inference, of course, is that Gad's Hill is relatively close to Wilson's. This is quite clearly the case in the manuscript version, in which Michaelis is told, when he wakes about 10:30, that Wilson "went out about an hour ago" (MS, p. 233);[61] two-and-a-half hours of slow walking would put Gad's Hill only five or six miles away at most.

But by the only workable scheme the final text allows, the emphasis of "he didn't reach Gad's Hill until noon" must be shifted, quite unnaturally, to the time he has been walking; and to cover nine or ten miles at a pace slow enough to be remarked, Wilson must be on the road for better than four hours, perhaps even five. He must begin sometime around 7:30, and keep walking, more or less continually, for a total of about seven-and-a-half hours. Quite a performance for a "spiritless" and "anaemic" fellow (p. 16).

The preceding paragraphs are littered with estimations, of course, but none of them, I think, can be more than a little inexact; and because of the four distinct stages of Wilson's journey, the inexactitudes do not accumulate. Needless to say, there is no real possibility that Fitzgerald plotted or timed the journey. His narrative invites the inference of a very long walk, but there is no hint that he was thinking of a feat of the order that is demanded by what we learn of the novel's geography and its clock.

For what it is worth, the "real" geography would simply aggravate the problem. From Flushing Meadows (Wilson's) to Manorhaven (Tom's) to King's Point (Gatsby's) is a literally staggering twenty-three miles. And Fitzgerald's grasp of Long Island geography seems even less firm than his control of the fictional locale: the manuscript has Wilson going to Tom's by way of Huntington, which is about twelve miles east of Manhasset Neck/East Egg (MS, p. 234).

Chapter 9 (The Funeral)

Seemingly, there is almost a week between the murder and the funeral. Five different days are adduced by the narrative, within which a rather large number of events occur. In general, they appear somewhat implausibly huddled together, and two or three last incoherences are suggested by their relationship.

The first of these days is, of course, the remainder of the Tuesday on which Gatsby dies: the police and the press appear, and Nick unsuccessfully phones both Daisy and Wolfsheim. The call to Wolfsheim is "long after five" (p. 110), which correlates with the time of Nick's discovery of the corpse in chapter 8.

The following day, Wednesday, on which "the newspaper reports next morning" (p. 109) appear, is also the day of the "next morning" (p. 110), when Nick and Wolfsheim exchange letters, and of "that afternoon" (p. 111), when Slagle calls from Chicago. It is a Wednesday only by extrapolation forward from the Saturday on which Gatsby's parties ended; there is in fact no further specification of days of the week after that point. It is extremely unlikely that Fitzgerald intended to locate these last events so precisely, but the narrative does logically require these placements.

Quite where the inquest can be fitted into this time scheme is almost impossible to imagine. Since it is narrated at the beginning of the chapter, before we learn of Nick's calls to Daisy and Wolfsheim on the evening of the murder, it is obviously out of the usual chronological sequence. It would seem that an inquest into a homicide should precede the release of the body for burial and that a couple of days of preparation—including some police investigation mentioned in chapter 8 (p. 107)—should precede the formal hearing. Yet there seems no room for such a lapse of time in Nick's account, and Gatsby's body has been returned and laid out in "the drawing-room" (p. 112) by the time his father arrives. As a matter of fact, his body was laid out in "the drawing-room" (p. 110) on the evening of the murder, and one suspects that Fitzgerald never imaginatively moved it.

But an absolute contradiction cannot be posited, because the next reference formally adduces doubt into the chronology: "I think it was on the third day that a telegram signed Henry C. Gatz arrived from a town in Minnesota" (p. 111). Even if Nick were not atypically unsure, "the third day" could be either literally three days after the murder—by extrapolation, Friday—or the third day of Nick's "taking responsibility" for Gatsby—thus, Thursday. The very opening of the chapter—"After two years I remember the rest of that day, and that night and the next day" (p. 109)—certainly allows for the possibility of taking the day of Gatsby's death as the "first" day.

Gatz himself arrives presumably one day after his telegram, since he claims that he "started right away," although the narrative specifies only a "warm September day" (p. 111) for his arrival. Incidentally, if he does arrive a day after his telegram, that is, on Friday or Saturday, the extrapolation process will result in an extreme unlikelihood, if not an absolute contradiction. On the day of Gatz's arrival, Nick tells Klipspringer, "The funeral's tomorrow," and on "the morning of the funeral" (p. 113), Nick visits Wolfsheim in his office, thus seemingly not on a Saturday or a Sunday. Admittedly, some people regularly work on Saturdays, and probably more did in 1922, but it is hard to imagine that Wolfsheim is one of them. "The Swastika Holding Company" (p. 113) is clearly just a front, and bootleggers who fix the World Series cannot be expected to put in forty-four hour weeks at the office.[62] It is well to remember that Nick simply presumes that Wolfsheim is in; he deliberately does not telephone.

There is also something huddled about the funeral arrangements. Shortly after Gatz arrives, Nick tells him that, as he had requested in his telegram, "all arrangements had been deferred until he came." Upon hearing this, Gatz has a brief conversation with Nick and goes "instantly asleep" (p. 112); yet by that evening, so Nick tells Klipspringer, the arrangements have been completed for "three o'clock" (p. 113) on the following day.[63]

The newspaper accounts of Gatsby's death also present some difficulty. We are told twice (pp. 109, 110) that the story appears in the next day's paper. This certainly means the New York papers, and it should not have been beyond the competence of journalism in 1922 for the story to make the afternoon Chicago papers as well. Yet Slagle, who should be aware of such things, is ignorant of Gatsby's death when he calls from Chicago that afternoon (p. 111).[64] On the other hand, the Chicago newspaper reports are how Gatz—in Minnesota—learned of his son's death: "I saw it in the Chicago newspaper, . . . It was all in the Chicago newspaper" (p. 111). One is left, I suppose, to choose whether it is more likely to take an extra day for the story to reach the Chicago papers or for the Chicago papers to reach Minnesota.

The three last events of chapter 9 all occur after the funeral and cause no chronological problems. Nick's last meeting with Jordan takes place shortly after he decides to go home, "when the blue smoke of brittle leaves was in the air and the wind blew the wet laundry stiff" (p. 118). Mid-October seems about right, since the chance meeting with Tom, which is narrated immediately after, is specifically located on "one afternoon late in October" (p. 119). Nick's visit to Gatsby's house "on the last night" (p. 121) should be about the beginning of November, which allows for Nick's claim at the opening of the novel that "I came back from the East last autumn" (p. 1). One hopes it is unseasonably warm, for Nick delivers the "boats against the current" coda while "sprawled out on the sand" (p. 121).

There is one last aspect of the novel's treatment of present chronology yet to be dealt with: the references to the "three months" of the summer, one of which occurs in each of the last three chapters. Like the more numerous references to the five years of Gatsby's devotion, these also emphasize the unity of a time frame, and further, they contrast the time frame's relative brevity to the number and critical quality of the things that have occurred within it. Thus, the "three months" references clearly are presented as approximations, not strict chronological measurements. Within this context, all are accurate enough.

In chapter 7, on the night of Myrtle's death, Nick reflects on the dinner party in chapter 1, "three months before" (p. 97); from the very end of August back to the first week or so of June, perhaps a week short of a literal three months. In chapter 8, on the morning of the murder, Nick recalls his first party at Gatsby's "three months before" (p. 103); this is somewhat less precise—from about the last day of August back to mid-June, almost exactly two-and-a-half months. And in chapter 9, at the funeral, Nick remembers meeting Owl Eyes at the same party, again "three months before" (p. 117). It is now, as the reference to Gatz's arrival demonstrates, early September, or literally about ten days less than three months from the party in mid-June.

The sense of relative brevity might have been intensified had Fitzgerald written "less than three months," which in fact is the case. He seems rather to be insisting more strongly on the completion, and hence the integrity, of the summer as a critical time frame. One cannot quarrel with this choice of emphasis, but it may be noted that by insisting that the three months of the summer is a humanly meaningful measure and that the summer as a whole is integral, Fitzgerald implicitly accepts the demands of portraying the passage of the summer and its parts in coherence to one another, and hence in proper chronology.

In summary, one must judge Fitzgerald's handling of the chronology of his novel's present time as something less than competent. In the early chapters, the reshuffling of summer events puts Myrtle's party out of temporal sequence, perhaps deceptively so; and, as a corollary, the "reading over" transition is made to refer to Gatsby's party as the third in a series of events of which it is actually the second. Moving the fourth chapter to late July requires both Gatsby and Jordan, quite out of character, to wait about five weeks before enlisting Nick in the planned reunion, and also misappropriates the tonality of the kiss in the victoria from a week or so after Nick meets Jordan to considerably more than a month. And the misappropriation is much compounded by placing the careless driver conversation at Warwick before the cab ride so that the romance becomes either chronologically or else emotionally impossible. In general, all these events appeared in the manuscript version at times and in sequences appropriate to their meanings; in the final text they are reordered or repositioned without sufficient coherence to one another or to the calendar.

In the sixth and seventh chapters, the much praised relocation of materials dealing with Gatsby's past is accompanied by faulty integrations into the summer time scheme, so that the opening of the earlier chapter is formally contradictory and the opening of the latter insolubly ambiguous. Beyond this, there are rather frequent examples of chronological weaknesses within chapters, as with the huddling of events in the final chapter, or of lapses produced by focusing too closely on the individual event, as with Nick's recalling his last party at Gatsby's "two weeks ago."

Some suggestions have already been made in passing about why various of these problems occurred. For the moment, just one observation may be reiterated: with the single exception of the acceleration of time on the day of Gatsby's death, no one of these discrepancies is a necessary means to a valid artistic end. To say the least, Tom would be no less successful a characterization for driving back from Wilson's in twenty minutes; the anticipation of Gatsby's appearance no less intense for avoiding the inclusion of subsequent events; the summer of 1922 no less compelling for being temporally coherent; and Nick no less effective a narrator for having a better sense of when things happened.

3

The Chronology of the Past

Having seen the problems in the novel's present chronology, one should not be surprised that there are similar incoherences in the management of the past time frame—predominantly that of Gatsby's five years of devotion to Daisy. On the whole, however, the discrepancies in the past time frame are rather less frequent and are less often related to Fitzgerald's revisions than those in the present. In part, this is merely the result of fewer incidents being posited in more spacious time frames, which lessens the likelihood of contradiction. The manuscript version, for example, alternatively places the beginning of Gatsby's adolescent romanticism in his fourteenth (MS, p. 163) and in his fifteenth (MS, p. 217) year; the final text cuts both references, but could have retained either, since it adduces nothing contradictory.

It also seems true, however, that Fitzgerald was somewhat more consistent and successful in his revisions of past time references. At the least, he attained complete coherence about two key datings: that Gatsby's romance with Daisy occurred in the fall, and that his devotion endured for five years. There are vestiges in the manuscript of earlier decisions on both matters: at two places the romance is located in the summer, and, in two others, three years of devotion is posited. There are also indications of what was probably a related plan to place the present action first in 1923, and then in 1921.[1] Nothing of these earlier intentions, so far as I can see, survives in the final text.

Fitzgerald's own biography seems to have influenced these earlier intentions. He resided in Great Neck/East Egg during the summer of 1923, and his experiences there provided the basis for much of the content of *Gatsby*, as Fitzgerald himself testified much later in his notes on the sources of the nine chapters.[2] And he had, of course, as a young lieutenant, met and fallen in love with Zelda Sayre in the summer of 1918. These facts seem to have dictated Fitzgerald's initial intention of a romance in the summer of 1918, and, hence, of five years of commitment to Daisy, ending in 1923.

I have no useful suggestion about why Fitzgerald then relocated the action in 1921, but it must have been this relocation that explains the references to a three-year commitment. No other hypothesis seems to make sense, for three years back from either 1922 or 1923 would put the romance after the War. The five-year period of the final text is indeed a more satisfactory warrant of Gatsby's devotion. Further, Fitzgerald seems to have developed a special fondness for the period of five years in this context, since, in two short stories written during the composition of *Gatsby*, he has unsuccessful lovers waiting for that length of time.[3]

The final text might suggest that Fitzgerald moved the romance from summer to fall for the atmospheric and symbolic resonance of "that mysterious excitement . . . which comes at the two changes of the year" (p. 74). It may well have been, however, that the fall of 1917 was chosen merely as a compromise between the summer of 1917—perhaps too early since America entered World War I only in April of that year—and the summer of 1918—perhaps too late to allow for Gatsby's heroics, as it was in fact too late to allow for the author's. In any case, with complete consistency and with even greater emphasis than the manuscript, the final text refers to the five-year commitment eight times (pp. 52, 57, 63, 72, 73, and three times on p. 87).[4]

Like the three months of the summer of 1922, Gatsby's five years are, strictly speaking, a bit less than that, for he dies perhaps five or six weeks before the fifth anniversary of his meeting Daisy. We know this with certainty since the time of their romance in the final text is frequently, and invariably consistently, placed in the fall. Jordan meets the lovers "one October day in nineteen-seventeen" (p. 49); at the reunion, Gatsby says it is "five years next November" (p. 57) since he has seen Daisy; the incarnation passage in chapter 6 is located on "one autumn night five years before" (p. 63); Gatsby's account in chapter 8 says that "he took Daisy one still October night" (p. 99) and puts the ending of "their month of love" on "a cold fall day" (p. 100). They are, incidentally, reunited for almost exactly a second "month of love," from the meeting at Nick's in very late July to Gatsby's death at the close of August. I suspect that, if Fitzgerald had been aware enough of his chronology to realize the situation, some mild irony on it would have been in the text.

Fitzgerald made firm decisions on when the romance took place and presented them with complete consistency throughout the novel. There is, however, a great deal in his chronology of the past that is otherwise.

Prior to Gatsby's meeting Daisy, we learn, and clearly are meant to learn, relatively little of the five major characters. Gatsby, the eldest of the five, was born "James Gatz of North Dakota" (p. 64), almost certainly in 1890 or late 1889. Nick, on first sight, thinks him "a man of about my age" (p. 31), which he quickly refines to "an elegant young roughneck a year or two over thirty" (p. 32). His age is corroborated by the information that "at the age of seventeen" (p. 64), he met Dan Cody "five years" (p. 66) after Cody's 1902 affair with Ella Kaye and, thus, in 1907. The photograph of Gatsby "in yachting costume . . . taken when he was about eighteen" (p. 62) also derives from his time with Cody; perhaps Fitzgerald intended it to belong to the very beginning, since, a few pages later, we hear of Cody's outfitting his new protégé with "a blue coat, six pairs of white duck trousers, and a yachting cap" (p. 66).

Fitzgerald had some second thoughts about Gatsby's age in the manuscript. At their first meeting, Nick thinks, "He was older than me" (MS, p. 53); but a few pages later, his outrage at Gatsby's arrogant summons of Jordan is all the greater because "he was this side of thirty—not a day older than me!" (MS, p. 57). In one of the sequences of the confrontation chapter, however, Gatsby expostulates, "I'm only thirty-two now" (MS, p. 176). This coincides with the book's final judgment on the matter, but the final judgment may have come a good deal later. After reading the typescript version of the novel, Perkins noted in his letter of 20 November 1924, that "a reader . . . gets an idea that Gatsby is a much older man than he is, although you have the writer say that he is little older than himself"; and Fitzgerald, around 20 December, replied that "the man I had in mind, half unconsciously, *was* older (specific individual) and evidently, without so much as a definate [sic] word, I conveyed the fact."[5] Gatsby's age in the final text may well be in part acknowledgement of this impression and, in part, a device to forestall the impression that he is much older.

Cody's patronage "lasted five years" (p. 66), until 1912, when he dies and Ella Kaye defrauds Gatsby, now evidently twenty-two, of his legacy.[6] From this time until the twenty-seven-year-old Gatsby meets Daisy in October 1917, we learn almost nothing. Nor apparently does Nick, for, in his paraphrase of Gatsby's account of the meeting, he says that Gatsby had met people of Daisy's class "in various unrelated capacities" (p. 99). Clearly they were subordinate capacities, since the Gatsby of the 1917 meeting is characterized as "a penniless young man without a past" (p. 99).

This last fact is a bit difficult to square with Gatsby's "I accepted a commission as first lieutenant when it began" (p. 43). How Gatsby, without money or connections, managed a commission as first lieutenant is puzzling. Fitzgerald—who was himself commissioned a second lieutenant and would have recognized the distinction—presumably decided to start Gatsby as first lieutenant to allow for his making major in about a year and a half. At a couple of places in the manuscript version (MS, pp. 71, 86 cancel), Gatsby is a second lieutenant.[7]

This information about his commission, incidentally, is provided by Gatsby himself on the ride to New York, during which he also tells of having collected rubies and hunted big game, and, in fact, even claims that he "tried very hard to die" in the War because of "something very sad that had happened . . . long ago" (p. 43). Yet all the other details of his military career prove true,[8] and the commission as first lieutenant suits well with the completely reliable report that "he was a captain before he went to the front" (p. 100), which, as will be seen, probably means by June of 1918.

There is greater difficulty with the earliest evidence about Gatsby's life—the schedule of resolves he wrote on the flyleaf of *Hopalong Cassidy* and dated "September 12, 1906" (p. 116). This scarcely leaves time for him to work on the shores of Lake Superior for "over a year" (p. 65) before meeting Cody, apparently sometime in 1907.[9] The young Gatsby had planned to follow his schedule in the environment of his home—note, for example, "Be better to parents" (p. 116)—and given his enormous willpower, we would imagine he did so for some time after 12 September 1906 and before "he run off from home" (p. 115). Yet "over a year" afterward, he meets Cody early enough in 1907 to be lounging—rather like Nick fifteen years later—on the beach "in a torn green jersey and a pair of canvas pants" (p. 65). Since "September 12, 1906" seems a totally arbitrary date, perhaps it is better to consider Fitzgerald unlucky rather than careless in having chosen it.

Nick's thirtieth birthday occurs on the day of the Plaza scene, so we know that he was born at the end of August 1892. We learn very little of his life before 1922: he graduated from Yale in 1915, fought in the War, and got into "that tangle back home" with the girl with the "faint mustache of perspiration" (p. 39). After his decision "to go East and learn the bond business," he reports with some amusement that "all my aunts and uncles talked it over as if they were choosing a prep school for me. . . . Father agreed to finance me for a year" (p. 2). The satire, however, may seem to reflect unconsciously back on Nick; his earlier life seems so scanty of undertaking or accomplishment as to suggest a mightily extended adolescence.[10]

It perhaps would be well here to state explicitly that I judge such adverse criticism of Nick to be a reasonable inference from the text, though all but totally unintended by Fitzgerald. As with his cavalier treatment of working hours and girls from Jersey City, Nick's seeming fecklessness is, I believe, the result of the author's lack of control of the overtones such narrative details can create in a novel so highly selective of what it portrays. The point is worth making since some criticism of Gatsby has insisted that we are intended to recognize Nick's shortcomings and critically distance ourselves from his moral judgments.[11] Although formally this study is interested in Nick only as factually, not morally, reliable narrator—and no one seems to have denied this—still, it is perhaps well to indicate its orientation on this matter.

Briefly, it seems to me quite certain that Fitzgerald intended Nick as the locus of decency and sanity in the novel. He is continually contrasted as the realist in opposition to the romantic Gatsby, yet he is romantic enough himself to discern the ultimate nobility of Gatsby's longing for the transcendent. He is sufficiently provincial and naive to be dazzled by the glamor he encounters and even to feel somewhat inferior, and he is, as his father taught him to be, initially tolerant. But he is also, as he says, essentially honest, and the moral judgments he finally comes to are those Fitzgerald intends us to share. Reading The Great Gatsby and somehow divorcing one's sympathies from the character who announces that Tom and Daisy are careless people and Gatsby worth the whole damn bunch of them seems to me an exercise in perversity.[12]

To return to the other major characters, there is also very little specific information about the young Tom Buchanan. Yet one feels no lack: casual brutality, chronic infidelity, being rich, playing polo, and latterly dreading the rise of the colored empires seem a full life for him. We are ignorant about his service in the War; properly so, I think. Elsewhere the novel suggests that only "the flat-footed, short-sighted young men" (p. 50) stayed home, so explaining why he did not serve could have been awkward. On the other hand, there is a commendable tact, whether conscious or instinctive, in Fitzgerald's unwillingness to admit Tom to the experience that initiates the bond between Gatsby and Nick.

The few specifics we do learn about Tom, however, present a temporal contradiction. On his first appearance, he is described by Nick as "a sturdy straw-haired man of thirty." Because the two "were in the same senior society" (p. 5), we would expect Nick to know Tom's age, and because for Nick thirty is a critically different age from twenty-nine, we would expect him to be exact. Yet he also characterizes Tom, because of his football prowess at Yale, as "one of those men who reach . . . an acute limited excellence at twenty-one" (p. 2). But if Tom was twenty-one when he graduated in the summer of 1915, he is only twenty-eight during the summer of 1922. And even if his reaching an acute limited excellence at twenty-one refers to his last football season in the fall of 1914, he is still only twenty-nine in the summer of 1922.[13]

We know the ages of the two girls fairly firmly. Jordan reports that, on "the October day in nineteen-seventeen" when she saw Gatsby and Daisy together, "she was just eighteen, two years older than me" (p. 49). Thus, Daisy's date of birth is about September 1899,[14] and Jordan's late 1901. Their youth is surprising. Daisy is only twenty-two when she tells Nick, "I've been everywhere and seen everything and done everything. . . . Sophisticated—God, I'm sophisticated!" (p. 12). For that matter, she is probably still only twenty-two when Gatsby dies. Jordan, for whose incurable dishonesty Nick rejects her, can barely be twenty-one at their last interview, and was only about seventeen when the near scandal about her cheating developed. It was "at her first big tournament" (p. 38), and Jordan says: "That was nineteen-seventeen. By the next year . . . I began to play in tournaments" (p. 50).

Female character seems irrevocably determined very early in life, but, for the male, Fitzgerald allows a more generous period to at least radically redirect his life and energies. Gatsby is twenty-seven when he chooses Daisy as the object of his aspirations, and nearly thirty when he begins to make his fortune through the partnership with Wolfsheim; Tom is about twenty-seven when he marries; and Nick is twenty-nine before, so far as we know, he even tentatively chooses a career. One suspects that Fitzgerald was constrained to make his male characters thirtyish to allow them the experience of college and then the War, but that, in his own imagination, women who would serve as romantic objects had to be in their early twenties at most. He was himself only twenty-six when he began *Gatsby*, and only twenty-eight when it was published.

On the other hand, the sluttish Myrtle is "in the middle thirties" (p. 16), about five years older than her lover. To judge from her giving up at death "the tremendous vitality she had stored so long" (p. 92), Fitzgerald perhaps thought this a rather advanced age for a woman.[15]

We are told nothing of Wilson's age, but it must be about the same as Myrtle's, to judge from the references to their married life. There are three of these, and they are completely consistent: Wilson tells Tom that Myrtle has been talking about going west "for ten years" (p. 80); Catherine tells Nick, "They've been living over that garage for eleven years" (p. 23); and Wilson tells Michaelis he has been married for "twelve years" (p. 105). One can even find a touch of marital comedy in the sequence, which just conceivably may have been conscious, since Fitzgerald revised the last reference from "fourteen years" (MS, p. 229).

The chronology of Gatsby's five-year commitment to Daisy is in largest part presented in two extended recapitulations. The first is Jordan's account in chapter 4, in which she tells Nick of Daisy's activities from the time of the romance to about mid-1921; the second is Gatsby's account (although formally Nick narrates almost all of it) in chapter 8 of his own experience from meeting Daisy until his stay at Oxford, when he receives her last letter. Thus, the crucial evidences about the five years are unlike those about the present, which are the testimony of the narrator, Nick. These are, either formally or effectively, the testimonies of other characters; and, therefore, their narrative method must be explored in some detail to establish the reliability of what they tell us about the chronology of the past.

Jordan's account provides a natural matrix for investigating this chronology, not just because it is the earliest, most comprehensive, and most detailed presentation of the events of these years, but also because there are strong evidences of its complete reliability. Since it occurs after about a third of the story has elapsed and removes, as Sklar says, the first "of the veils from Gatsby's mystery,"[16] the sheer narrative impetus of the novel validates it. More important, the method of narration does so as well. Jordan's account is presented as her verbatim testimony and is

the only example in the novel of extended narration by a character other than Nick. That her testimony is authoritative is established by her recreation of three key scenes to which she was an
eyewitness: the meeting with the lovers in Louisville, the sober-
ing-up of Daisy on the evening of her bridal dinner, and the visit
with the newly wed Buchanans. Each scene is firmly set in time
and place, and the accuracy of Jordan's recollection is endorsed
by her relation of quite specific, sometimes even inconsequential,
details.

The first scene, one "October day in nineteen-seventeen,"
opens with Jordan whimsically aware of her "shoes from England
with rubber knobs on the soles" and her "new plaid skirt which
blew a little in the wind," and moves to her meeting the lovers
in Daisy's "white roadster . . . beside the curb" (p. 49) in front of
her house. The scene of Daisy's drunkenness begins when Jordan
"came into her room half an hour before the bridal dinner, and
found her lying on her bed as lovely as the June night—and as
drunk as a monkey," and continues with such notable particularities as the bottle of sauterne, the string of pearls in the waste
basket, and Gatsby's letter, "squeezed . . . up into a wet ball"
(p. 50) and disintegrating in the bath water. The last scene is "in
Santa Barbara" and "in August," and deals with customary,
rather than particular, details; but these—such as Daisy's uneasy
"Where's Tom?" or her fondness for "rubbing her fingers over his
eyes" (p. 51)—are sufficiently individuated to continue the effect
of Jordan's accuracy and reliability. Further, the transitional passages between these scenes support the effect by being continually definite about time and, at least frequently—the reference to
Tom's accident, for example—specific in detail.

What has been described here as the method of Jordan's narration in chapter 4 is, in peto, the method of Nick's narration of the
novel as a whole—"a series of scenes dramatizing the important
events of the story and connected by brief passages of interpretation and summary."[17] That correspondence itself further attests
that Fitzgerald intended Jordan's account to be considered authoritative.

Pragmatically, it might also be said that, since the very fact
of Jordan's narrating implies the necessity to the narrative of
information which at the moment only she possesses, there is
by definition no perspective from which that information may
be demonstrated to be wrong. Jordan's account simply becomes
Nick's narrative, with no critical disassociation on his part before
or after and no interruption beyond a parenthesis in the first

sentence to establish the provenance of the account. Both Miller and Perosa speak of Jordan's function here as that of a *ficelle*, in the manner of Henry James, whose dramatic justification in the narrative is a technical problem of some complexity, but the reliability of whose testimony is implicitly beyond question.[18]

Gatsby's account in chapter 8 of his own activities, which, together with a number of random passages, is to be measured against Jordan's, has at the very least an equal warrant of reliability. In terms of the narrative's impetus, it is here finally (to borrow again from Sklar) that "the remaining veils come off Gatsby's mystery,"[19] and Nick, and we, obtain the last pieces to complete the puzzle, to understand the novel's hero, and to validate the title's assertion of his greatness.

The narrative technique of the section is extremely complicated and relates critically to the thematic core of the novel. Thus, it requires a considerable digression to establish the issues with which it deals and the methods by which it communicates.

There is in the novel a very special problem created by the characterization of its hero. The story posits in Gatsby a yearning for and perhaps even a capacity to touch the infinite, but, just as surely, it presents a Gatsby totally incapable of articulating his aspirations or his experience.

As a number of commentators have noted, Gatsby speaks relatively little in the novel; in fact, he speaks less at each level of Fitzgerald's composition. In the final text, what he does say is basically of two kinds. When he is most self-conscious of his own image as Jay Gatsby, he affects—as Nick notes at their first meeting—an "elaborate formality of speech that just missed being absurd" (p. 32). His talk on the ride to New York is much in this vein; "old sport" is its perfect adumbration. Often, however, under the stress of emotion or in his intimacy with Nick, he expresses himself quite simply—with no rhetorical flourishes, with no lexical or syntactical sophistication. Often his sentences are clumsily repetitious; often he includes irrelevant detail. He is a man who has no skill in speech, and he fails miserably when he tries to defend himself verbally in the Plaza scene.

Even when he comes closest to expressing his vision, he does so in a stark, absolute, abrupt speech that startles or puzzles Nick: "Can't repeat the past? . . . Why of course you can!" (p. 73); or, on Daisy's ultimate attraction, "Her voice is full of money" (p. 80); or, on her loving Tom, "In any case . . . it was just personal" (p. 101). Lionel Trilling has perceptively commented on "the intellectual audacity" of this last statement, claiming that it confers on Gatsby a kind of "insane greatness."[20] But in neither his idiom as mad philosopher nor his idiom as self-advertising success can Gatsby's language evoke Gatsby's experience, and he is in fact a kind of inarticulate poet. He attempts to communicate his vision by his devotion to Daisy, his wealth, his house, his parties, even his shirts. And it is just this—that beneath the gaudy and absurdly inadequate structures he erects, his vision is genuine—that Nick, and Fitzgerald, find fascinating and noble.

But Gatsby's longing for transcendence must be expressed in words in the novel, and it falls to Nick to express it. Yet, in spite of Nick's undergraduate dabbling in literature, his wit, and even his sensitivity to mood and emotion, it is not quite completely in character for him to do so. For Nick, more than anything else, is realism set against Gatsby's romanticism. Within that realism there is, to be sure, sufficient thwarted or potential or empathetic romanticism to respond to Gatsby, but it is the very fact that Gatsby's experience is beyond him that makes it for Nick wondrous and worthy to record.

There are a number of points in the novel where Gatsby's wondrous experience enters the narrative, paradoxically as experienced by Gatsby but as rendered by Nick. A very neat instance is the poeticizing that is triggered by Gatsby's "Her voice is full of money"; Nick reflects:

That was it. I'd never understood before. It was full of money—that was the inexhaustible charm that rose and fell in it, the jingle of it, the cymbals' song of it. . . . High in a white palace the king's daughter, the golden girl. . . .

(p. 80)

In a very brief compass, we have here both Nick's lyric evocation and the stimulus Gatsby provided to inspire it. But the case is somewhat atypical, for the novel nowhere else, I think, specifies exactly what Gatsby tells Nick to justify what Nick tells us; and it might also be argued that the perception of Daisy's charm—the theme of this small rhapsody—is not Gatsby's unique experience, but one shared by many men, including Nick himself.

The passage on Gatsby's leaving the Louisville that Daisy "had made lovely for him" (p. 102) is more characteristic of Nick's lyric recreations of Gatsby's experience, but that passage will be discussed later in another connection. Here, the process will be investigated in regard to two other sections of the novel: one, of course, is the account in chapter 8 of Gatsby's affairs, which is crucial to the book's chronology of the past; the second—the more impassioned and ultimately the less successful—is the closing of chapter 6, which I have referred to as the incarnation passage.

That passage follows the conversation after the second party in which Gatsby insists to Nick that the past can be repeated. Just prior to the incarnation passage is a brief paragraph beginning, "He talked a lot about the past," which establishes Gatsby as the ultimate source of what is to come. The paragraph closes with a sentence, which, in its struggling simplicity and vagueness, convincingly suggests Gatsby's experience in Gatsby's words: "His life had been confused and disordered since then, but if he could once return to a certain starting place and go over it all slowly, he could find out what that thing was. . . ." (p. 73).

Then, with no transition but a second ellipsis, the scene moves to "one autumn night, five years before," and we have two paragraphs filled with the most heightened, impassioned, and lyrical detail in the novel: the "mysterious excitement" of the change of season, the ladder mounting "to a secret place above the trees," "the incomparable milk of wonder," the wedding of "his unutterable visions to her perishable breath," "the tuning-fork that had been struck on a star," and the climactic detail—"she blossomed for him like a flower and the incarnation was complete" (pp. 73–74).

For two paragraphs, the narrative has become the evocation of Gatsby's quasi-mystical experience largely through the imagery of nature, the cosmos, and the divine; therefore, presumably Nick has become lyric poet. Then, however, comes the closing paragraph of the chapter, beginning, "Through all he said, even through his appalling sentimentality, I was reminded of something" (p. 74); and for the balance of the paragraph, Nick struggles and fails to capture his own fleeting or forgotten intimation of the transcendent.

The return from Gatsby's incarnation of his vision to Nick's more mundane sensibility is managed well enough; and, if there is an implicit contradiction in Nick's inability to feel as participant what he has himself as narrator just evoked, perhaps the problem of concreticizing Gatsby's experience admits of no better solution. But Nick's opening—"Through all he said, even through his appalling sentimentality"—strikes a particularly false note. For surely we are not meant to think of the two paragraphs that precede either as what Gatsby said or as appallingly sentimental. Insofar as they are anybody's speech, they are Nick's, and the disassociation from them is far too abrupt.

The sentence in question is an unfortunate case of Fitzgerald's fondness for salvaging and relocating elements from earlier drafts. In manuscript, it is after Gatsby sings the song he wrote when he was fourteen that Nick says, "through all he said, even through the doggerel of the song, I was reminded of something" (MS, p. 163). The song is, both objectively and in Nick's judgment, appallingly sentimental, but such a characterization is simply not automatically transferable to the incarnation paragraphs in the final text.

Gatsby's song, by the way, represents an alternative attempt in the manuscript to concretize his vision within the text. Though mere doggerel to Nick, it is apparently to Gatsby an ideal expression of that vision, for he says, "the sound of it makes me perfectly happy." He even adds, quite charmingly, "But I don't sing it often now because I'm afraid I'll use it up" (MS, p. 163). But the validity of Gatsby's vision, one expects, would hardly have survived his verbal construct, and Fitzgerald wisely discarded the idea of Gatsby as his own lyricist.

He also discarded another, quite opposite, approach. Immediately after a version of the incarnation paragraphs that is substantially the same as the final text, the manuscript has the following:

> . . . He didn't really say any of this. What he said was that she had been an "ideal" of his, and that he'd never have such ideas about things or girls any more.
>
> (MS, p. 161)

This is much like the technique observed in Nick's response to Gatsby's "Her voice is full of money." The text provides not only Nick's imaginative elaboration, but also its literal basis in Gatsby's words. Here, however, there is such a chasm between Gatsby's prosaic scrap and the soaring lyricism which precedes it that Nick seems absurdly eccentric to have flown off into the mystical beyond. It is well within Gatsby's capacity to speak of Daisy as his ideal, but to so insist on the authenticity of his experience by presenting it as he would verbalize it robs the narrative of justification for the lyricism and robs the narrator of his reliability.

Yet all these elements were essential: the experience had to be authentically Gatsby's, it had to be rendered lyrically, and Nick's reliability as narrator had to be preserved. Given the difficulties, the closing of chapter 6 succeeds reasonably well; in chapter 8 much the same difficulties obtain, but the narration achieves even more—and even more successfully.

The key passage in chapter 8 is much longer: in toto, it is eleven paragraphs, broken typographically into three sections. As with the incarnation passage, it is preceded by a conversation between Nick and Gatsby; it is now very early on the morning of the murder, and Gatsby has just told Nick "the strange story of his youth with Dan Cody" (p. 98). And even more clearly than with the incarnation passage, we are assured that Gatsby himself is the ultimate source of what will follow: the prefatory material ends with "but he wanted to talk about Daisy" (p. 99).

The first of the three sections of the chapter 8 account is a sequence of five paragraphs relating Gatsby's meeting Daisy, "taking" her, and then, to his surprise, finding himself irrevocably committed to her. The emphasis, however, is far less on external event than on the precise affective quality of Gatsby's enchantment with Daisy and her world. Thus, we are again dealing with a kind of experience beyond Gatsby's power to recreate. It is, however, recreated, largely by romantic and imaginative vocabulary and detail: the "ripe mystery" of Daisy's house, the air pervaded "with the shades and echoes of still vibrant emotions" of her other suitors, "the invisible cloak" of Gatsby's uniform, his commitment "to the following of a grail," "the bought luxury of star-shine," and "Daisy, gleaming like silver, safe and proud above the hot struggles of the poor" (pp. 99–100).

Yet as well as establishing the precise quality of the experience, this section is much concerned with establishing its authenticity as Gatsby's experience as well. It achieves this by interspersing, within the heightened and evocative portrayal, sentences of sufficient simplicity and directness to suggest Gatsby's reactions as Gatsby might have phrased them: "It amazed him—he had never been in such a beautiful house before"; "But he didn't despise himself and it didn't turn out as he had imagined"; and, very much in his reductive idiom—"He felt married to her, that was all" (p. 99). Something of Gatsby's sense of being overwhelmed by this new ambience is neatly conveyed by the rhetorical tricks of polysyndeton and anaphora: "a hint of bedrooms upstairs more beautiful and cool than other bedrooms, of gay and radiant activities taking place through its corridors, and of romances that were not musty and laid away already in lavender, but fresh and breathing and redolent of this year's shining motor-cars and of dances whose flowers were scarcely withered" (p. 99).[21] Even the sense of Nick as narrator is included: "I don't mean that he had traded on his phantom millions"; "He had intended, probably, to take what he could and go—but now he found that he had committed himself to the following of a grail" (p. 99). Note in Nick's "probably" the reliability of the narrator who qualifies because he is not completely sure; note in "the following of a grail," the implication of a sensibility capable of translating Gatsby's experience into properly evocative imagery. The modulation among these several demands is commendably well done; the quality of the experience is rendered, it is convincingly tied to Gatsby, and the reliability and sensibility of the narrative voice are assured.

The second section of the chapter 8 account consists of just two paragraphs. The first is direct quotation from Gatsby, completely in his idiom (including an "old sport"), and reemphasizing the authenticity of the experience. The reemphasis is judicious, for the second paragraph is a tranquil, almost hushed recreation of the lovers' last day together. It contains details that it would be grotesque to think Gatsby had literally told Nick, such as Gatsby's changing the position of his arm as Daisy moved or Daisy's brushing "silent lips against his shoulder" (p. 100). But, by this time, the narrative technique has developed sufficient momentum that, as long as the effect of the details is a persuasive evocation of the emotional quality of the experience, we do not question how Nick could have obtained them. And there is no reminder in this section of Nick as narrator to tempt us to do so.

The final section of the chapter 8 account exploits this advantage to the fullest. The first of its four paragraphs begins with a brief recapitulation of Gatsby's exploits in the War, then moves to his being sent to Oxford, and to his emotions: "he tried frantically to get home." At this point, it makes a remarkable transition: "He was worried now—there was a quality of nervous despair in Daisy's letters. She didn't see why he couldn't come" (p. 100). And for the rest of the account, it is Daisy's experience that is recreated.

Nick, of course, has no source of any of this. The entire account has developed out of Gatsby's wanting "to talk about Daisy," but he does not know the minutiae of her experience any more than Nick does. Fitzgerald works an eminently successful bit of sleight of hand here: he manages to continue the warrant of authenticity the account has developed with regard to Gatsby into the recreation of Daisy's affairs.

As with Gatsby's, the mood of her experience is captured by striking and romantic images—orchestras "summing up the sadness and suggestiveness of life" and "rose petals blown by the sad horns around the floor"; as with Gatsby's experience, the intensity of Daisy's is suggested rhetorically: "She wanted her life shaped now, immediately—and the decision must be made by some force—of love, of money, of unquestionable practicality—that was close at hand" (p. 101). There is also a certain intensifying of the sense that this is indeed Daisy's experience, which is achieved in each of the two long paragraphs on her seduction by "her artificial world" by naming her only in the first clause of the paragraph and using personal pronouns exclusively thereafter.

The last, brief paragraph of the account ends the external events with the arrival of Tom. It reports Daisy's response—"There was a wholesome bulkiness about his person and position, and Daisy was flattered"; and then reminds us of our reliable narrator—"Doubtless there was a certain struggle and a certain relief"; and closes with a return to our ostensible and unimpeachable ultimate source: "The letter reached Gatsby while he was still at Oxford" (p. 101).

The use of Nick to provide a modified first-person narration in the style of Conrad has been perceptively analyzed by Miller.[22] But none of the standard methods he proposes explains what is happening in the chapter 8 account. It is, of course, not Nick's eyewitness testimony; nor is it, like the representation of Wilson's journey, pieced together from various sources; nor even, like the conversation between Wilson and Michaelis, is it implicitly derived from a participant, or, as Garrett suggests, from newspaper accounts.[23] Gatsby has undoubtedly told Nick something of the initial impact of Daisy's world, which may justify Nick's romantic embroidering that opens the chapter 8 account, but, even in these terms, there is no explanation of the information about Daisy's being seduced by her artificial world and won by Tom. One imagines she would have told Gatsby something about this time of her life, and, much less surely, Gatsby may have passed some part of it on to Nick. But the characterization of Daisy argues that she neither understood nor could have communicated her experience: she has little sensitivity, virtually no power of self-analysis, and, apart from a kind of practiced archness, no special skill in speech.

And even if she had, the testimony of the text unmistakably insists that Gatsby has no understanding of her experience *qua* her experience. Up until the confrontation, Gatsby believes as he tells Tom, "She only married you because I was poor and she was tired of waiting for me. It was a terrible mistake, but in her heart she never loved any one except me!" (p. 87). Even after Daisy fails him, he claims, "Of course she might have loved him just for a minute, when they were first married—and loved me more even then, do you see? . . . In any case . . . it was just personal" (p. 101). Even if Daisy could have created the precise affective quality of her experience for Gatsby, he could never have recreated it for Nick; and, thus, Nick has no plausible source for the paragraphs on Daisy.

Yet the narrative does indeed posit the precise affective quality of Daisy's experience at the end of the chapter 8 account, just as it posits the precise affective quality of Gatsby's at the beginning. Clearly, the recreation of such affective quality when the recreation is beyond the capacities of either character who underwent the experience is not the ordinary province of the first-person narrator. And although throughout most of *The Great Gatsby*, Nick's reliability as narrator and at least some implication of his access to information are carefully preserved, here his narration verges on the function of the omniscient author.

Although Miller does not focus on this section of the novel, he has admirably demonstrated Fitzgerald's intentions here:

> What Fitzgerald says of Cecilia, in his notes to *The Last Tycoon*, might well apply to Nick in *The Great Gatsby*: "by making Cecilia, at the moment of her telling the story, an intelligent and observant woman, I shall grant myself the privilege, as Conrad did, of letting her imagine the actions of the characters. Thus, I hope to get the verisimilitude of a first person narrative, combined with a Godlike knowledge of all events that happen to my characters." Fitzgerald could have substituted his own name for Conrad's had he recalled Nick Carraway.[24]

Because in the chapter 8 account Fitzgerald manages to transfer the establishment of the authenticity and the precise quality of one character's experience to that of another's, I think there is no better example of his modifying his first-person narration in the direction of authorial omniscience.

But to return to the significance of the chapter 8 account to the novel's chronology of the past, what is reported here, although ostensibly Gatsby is the ultimate source, has for all practical purposes the assurance of omniscience. The question of the artistic propriety of Fitzgerald's doing so is a subject of dispute among commentators, just two of whom will be mentioned here. Garrett, some of whose ideas have already been presented, sees the matter in terms of style and effect. He finds that the device of Nick as author (not just narrator) provides him with such abundant linguistic resources, generated by the interplay between the written and spoken vernacular, that, with the strong reminders "of the story as artifact, . . . ironically, it is Carraway's selective virtuosity that at once supersedes and disguises Fitzgerald's."[25] By the time we reach the passage on Gatsby's adolescent fantasizing in chapter 6, Garrett claims that "Carraway so dominates the material of the story . . . that he is capable of creating a language that can dramatize in rhythmic images the inward and spiritual condition of Gatsby as a young man" ("But his heart was in a constant, turbulent riot . . . ," p. 119); and that, in the last chapter, with Nick's imagining of dialogue from the dead Gatsby ("Look here, old sport, you've got to get somebody for me," p. 198), we have "this extension of style to the extreme, almost absurd edge of credibility."[26]

Ron Neuhaus presents a completely negative judgment of the matter, although, interestingly, like Garrett he begins with a perception of the book's style. Neuhaus is greatly displeased, if not actually offended, by some of Nick's more arch and inflated jocularities in the opening paragraphs, and claims that they establish "a sensibility that increasingly distances itself from literal reality by inflated rhetoric." As a result, "we reject Carraway's pompous moralizing after the first few paragraphs, and his reliability as a witness by the end of the second chapter."[27] From this point of view, it is completely to be expected that Neuhaus finds the language in which Nick presents the incarnation passage or, here in chapter 8, the materials on Daisy's experience to be culpably false and self-indulgent; Nick's speculations on Gatsby's final thoughts are, for Neuhaus, "an ooze of saccharine rhetoric."[28] He charges Fitzgerald with "attempting by attributive rhetoric to supply what characterization does not," finds that "the shifts in perspective destroy any integrity in the fiction," and assigns an ultimate cause for Fitzgerald's failure in the use of authorial omniscience: "because he cannot develop characters adequate to his vision of what those characters should be."[29]

It seems to me that Neuhaus is egregiously insensitive, if not actively hostile, to the tonalities of Fitzgerald's (and Nick's) prose, but, if it were as continually false and empty as he claims, the ultimate failure of the book would indeed be its concomitant. Obviously, my own views are closer to those of Garrett, who finds the novel's language varied, purposeful, and effective, although it seems to me (as it may not to Garrett) that there are moments when Fitzgerald's style can justly be seen as inflated and florid.

The more salient point for my own argument, however, is simply to note in these two diametrically opposed readings of Gatsby a common agreement on Fitzgerald's device of extending Nick's first-person retrospective into the realm of authorial omniscience. To question any part of Nick's credibility as narrator here—especially in regard to Daisy's experience, for which he has no plausible source—is to make nonsense of the narrative technique of the entire chapter 8 account.

Both Jordan's account in chapter 4, and what—largely as a rhetorical facility—has been referred to as Gatsby's account in chapter 8 are presented in the novel as unimpeachably reliable information. Thus, any contradiction between these two most salient evidences of the novel's past time would be a quite significant lapse in verisimilitude. As surely will be expected, such contradiction does in fact occur.

The five-year time frame of Gatsby's devotion begins with the romance in October and November of 1917, and the references to it in Jordan's account in chapter 4, in Gatsby's in chapter 8, and everywhere else in the novel are completely consistent. There is, however, at least a discrepancy immediately after.

Jordan reports a rumor about Daisy's "packing her bag one winter night to go to New York and say good-by to a soldier who was going overseas" (p. 50). Obviously this is the winter of 1917–18, and probably in January or February, since Jordan relates it in a paragraph dealing with the events of "next year."[30] But in Gatsby's account, his last meeting with Daisy, in November of 1917, is "on the last afternoon before he went abroad" (p. 100). Since it was impossible literally to go abroad from Louisville before the age of intercontinental air travel, this may be considered no more than a colloquial looseness of expression. Still, the two passages do suggest that, when Fitzgerald wrote them, he was thinking rather differently about when Gatsby sailed for France.

Gatsby's wartime exploits occur, of course, in 1918, and they are referred to at three places in the narrative. In chapter 3, on their first meeting, Gatsby and Nick identify their military units for each other. In chapter 4, during the ride to New York, Gatsby gives a rather melodramatic summary, including an account of his heroism in the Argonne commanding "two machine gun de-

tachments," and of his subsequent promotion to major and deco-
ration by "every allied government . . . even Montenegro" (p. 43).
In the chapter 8 account, there is a single, more prosaic statement: "He was a captain before he went to the front, and following the Argonne battles he got his majority and the command of
the divisional machine-guns" (p. 100).

Generally, the three passages form a consistent pattern, but
there are a number of anomalies, and, perhaps, a rather curious
error. The latter derives from the textual history of two of these
passages, which is possible to trace only because of Bruccoli's
admirable work in providing the apparatus for a definitive edition of Gatsby. In the cases of both the discussion of Nick's and
Gatsby's units in chapter 3 and the report of Gatsby's command
of "two machine-gun detachments" in chapter 4, the received
text of the novel is not that of the first edition. (This is, incidentally, a unique problem for this study: with none of the many
other passages examined here is there a relevant difference between the first edition and the subsequently received text.) In
the first edition—and in all the drafts—Gatsby asks whether Nick
served in the "First Division," Nick identifies his unit as the
"Twenty eighth Infantry," and Gatsby his as the "Sixteenth" Infantry. In his own copy of the first edition, however, Fitzgerald
changed the units to the "Third Division," the "Ninth Machine-
Gun Battalion," and the "Seventh Infantry," respectively, and the
changes were first incorporated in the published text in 1953.[31]
The provenance is exactly the same for the change from the first
edition's "the remains of my machine-gun battalion," which
Gatsby commanded in the Argonne to the received text's "two
machine-gun detachments."[32]

The purposes of these changes have, I believe, been correctly
discerned by Bruccoli. As he says, "The decrease in Gatsby's
command from a battalion to two detachments serves to emphasize his heroism"; and, as his notes make clear, the revision of
the units is an attempt at greater authenticity.[33] Nick's Ninth Machine-Gun Battalion and Gatsby's Seventh Infantry Regiment
were in fact components of the Third Division, and both did
indeed see action from late May to early July of 1918 around
Château-Thierry, in the first large-scale engagement of American
units in World War I. Since Fitzgerald seems to allude to that
engagement, it appears that he did some researching for these
revisions. Gatsby says that he served in the Seventh Infantry "until June nineteen-eighteen" (p. 31), which points to the allusion.
But the "until" is quite odd since the inference it invites is that

Gatsby left his unit just before or just after the fighting at Châ-teau-Thierry began, which can hardly be the novel's intention.

Gatsby's greatest achievements, however, were in the Argonne campaign, in October and November of 1918. His heroism there, according to the testimony in both chapter 4 and chapter 8, won him promotion to major and, according to the latter passage, also gained him "the command of the divisional machine-guns" (p. 100). But, as Bruccoli notes, the Third Division fought at the opposite end of the Meuse-Argonne offensive line, not in the Argonne itself.[34] Just conceivably, Gatsby's service in "the Sev-enth Infantry until June nineteen-eighteen" might be construed as his transferring out of the Third Division before the Argonne campaign. But in any case, since that campaign continued until the Armistice on 11 November 1918, Gatsby's winning command of the divisional machine-guns becomes a curiously pointless achievement, for there was no more fighting.[35]

What is most surprising, however, is that, in spite of the re-peated connection of Gatsby with machine-gun units, it is Nick, not he, who served in the Ninth Machine-Gun Battalion. Their shared experience as combat soldiers offers a sufficient begin-ning for their friendship; there seems no point to making them both experts with rapid-fire weapons, nor does the narrative make anything of it.

Moreover, if at some point Gatsby was in "command of the divisional machine-guns," it would seem to require, according to the actual military organization to which Fitzgerald alludes, that he had overall command of the three machine-gun battalions assigned to the Third Division—the Seventh, the Eighth, and the Ninth, Nick's unit. Thus, he would have stood in the chain of command immediately above the commanding officer of Nick's battalion. Nick—a Yale man—must have served as an officer, and his talk of enjoying the "counter-raid" (p. 2) establishes that he served through the final campaigns, when Gatsby won his hon-ors. Obviously, Nick ought to have known Gatsby in France, at least by name and reputation, but just as obviously, no such previous knowledge lies behind their first conversation.

The implications of putting Nick in the Ninth Machine-Gun Battalion are so strangely counterproductive that I very much suspect that Fitzgerald erred in revising the text of the first edi-tion; that what he intended was to put Gatsby in that unit and Nick in the Seventh Infantry. Such a revision would have been an attempt at greater coherence, for in spite of the recurrent asso-ciation of Gatsby with machine-gun units, the text of the first edition assigns him to the Sixteenth Infantry. Yet it is hard to believe that an infantry officer would be given command of the divisional machine-guns or would talk of holding out until "the infantry came up at last" (p. 43); and it is literally contradictory for an infantry officer to speak, as Gatsby does in the first edition, of "the remains of my machine-gun battalion" (italics added). It would have made little or no sense to put Nick in the Ninth Machine-Gun Battalion, but eminently good sense to place Gatsby there, and this I surmise is what Fitzgerald attempted to do, and then inadvertently transposed the two units.

Admittedly, the error that I am hypothesizing would have been a remarkable one—and all the more remarkable for not having been made under the pressure of imminent publication, which obtained in the case of every other incoherence noted in this study. The text of the first edition of *Gatsby* illustrates:

> "Your face is familiar," he said politely. "Weren't you in the First Division during the war?"
>
> "Why, yes, I was in the Twenty-eighth infantry."
>
> "I was in the Sixteenth until June nineteen-eighteen. I knew I'd seen you somewhere before."

Nick and Gatsby identify their units in consecutive and unattributed speeches; and if, as I suggest, Fitzgerald confused the units in his revision, he must have lost track of which speech belonged to which character. Every reader has experienced this problem at some time with unattributed dialogue, although here the "he said" just a couple of lines above (one would think) should have maintained the orientation of the exchange. Still, the carelessness and the extremely narrow focus of others of Fitzgerald's revisions argue that he was capable of even so remarkable an error as transposing the two units. If I am mistaken in this matter, then he simply introduced some pointless incoherence and the impossible implication that Nick should have known Gatsby during the War.

Jordan's account in chapter 4 sketches in rather rapidly Daisy's activities from her parting with Gatsby to her marriage. After she is "effectually prevented" by her family from seeing him off in New York, and subsequently is angry with them "for several weeks," she strikes a kind of compromise between absolute fidelity and social activity: "After that she didn't play around with the soldiers any more, but only with a few flat-footed, short-sighted young men in town, who couldn't get into the army at all" (p. 50), and who posed no romantic jeopardy.

But Jordan's paragraph immediately following presents, without comment, a Daisy whose commitment to Gatsby seems totally forgotten: "By the next autumn [1918] she was gay again, gay as ever. She had a debut after the Armistice, and in February she was presumably engaged to a man from New Orleans. In June she married Tom Buchanan with more pomp and circumstance than Louisville ever knew before" (p. 50). There are two subsequent references that refine this outline a bit. At the close of Gatsby's account in chapter 8, Tom arrives in Louisville "in the middle of the spring" (p. 101); in accord with Fitzgerald's customary usage and to allow time for the courtship and the plans for an elaborate wedding, his arrival should be about April of 1919. And in the Plaza scene, Daisy recalls that she was married "in the middle of June" (p. 84).

In contrast to Jordan's narrative, however, the account in chapter 8 places the beginning of Daisy's break with Gatsby during his time at Oxford, and creates two serious problems. The first has to do with why he was there. Gatsby invariably attempts to trade on his Oxford experience as if it were a credential of his attainment. He tries to impress Nick on the ride to New York and, after he displays his photo with the Earl of Doncaster (p. 44), Nick naively believes him. He has earlier made claims about Oxford to Jordan, who is incredulous (p. 32), and to Wolfsheim, who is immensely appreciative (pp. 47, 114). Even in the Plaza scene, when Gatsby provides the literal truth of his attendance— "It was nineteen-nineteen. I only stayed five months"—and his veracity is endorsed by Nick's wanting "to get up and slap him on the back," still he speaks of Oxford much as he had earlier, as if it were a main chance that had come his way: "It was an opportunity they gave to some of the officers after the Armistice. . . . We could go to any of the universities in England or France" (p. 86).

The implication—and in Daisy's presence—that he chose to attend Oxford rather than return to her is astonishing, and is explicitly contradicted by the authoritative presentation in chapter 8 of the relevant circumstances and feelings; "After the Armistice he tried frantically to get home, but some complication or misunderstanding sent him to Oxford instead" (p. 100). This is totally at odds with the idea of opportunities being provided to some fortunate officers or choices being made from among any of the universities in England or France. Gatsby's statement during the Plaza scene was moved to that position during Fitzgerald's revision of the galleys, and the implicit contradiction is aggravated by having him speak in Daisy's presence. But the basic incoherence existed in the earlier versions, in which, shortly before his long autobiographical account in chapter 8, Gatsby tells Nick: "No, I studied there—for six months. Perhaps you remember that a lot of American officers were given a chance to go there just after the war" (MS, p. 216).[36]

For Gatsby to have seized the chance to attend Oxford, one must suppose he no longer had hopes of winning Daisy, that she had already broken with him. But no substantiation exists in the novel beyond Gatsby's curious claim of having tried to die in the War, nor, so far as I can see, do the earlier drafts contain any evidence of such an intention. Daisy's final break with Gatsby, in both Jordan's narrative in chapter 4 and Gatsby's in chapter 8, occurs during his time at Oxford. But they are in total disagreement about the initiation and the progress of her disloyalty—the second and far more troublesome problem.

Immediately after placing Gatsby at Oxford, the account in chapter 8 continues: "he was worried now—there was a quality of nervous despair in Daisy's letters. She didn't see why he couldn't come. She was feeling the pressure of the world outside" (p. 100). The next two paragraphs trace this pressure on Daisy, the second of them beginning: "Through this twilight universe Daisy began to move again with the season." The process is completed in a brief final paragraph: "That force took shape in the middle of the spring with the arrival of Tom Buchanan. . . . The letter reached Gatsby while he was still at Oxford" (p. 101).

According to this account, Daisy remained faithful for some time after Gatsby's arrival at Oxford. Her letters in January or February of 1919—whichever was the first of his five months there—show only "a nervous despair," which, by clear implication, had not been present for the first thirteen months or so of their separation. Her beginning "to move again with the season" may refer only to a season of postwar revelry, but, if it does refer to the calendar, the season must be the spring of 1919. By this time, the pressures of her world have only begun to seduce her, and she does not acquiesce until after Tom arrives about April. Her letter breaking with Gatsby should date from May, for it elicits the letter she drunkenly clutches on the night of her bridal dinner in June.

In complete variance, Jordan's account in chapter 4 reports, "By next autumn she was gay again, gay as ever" (p. 50). This is the autumn of 1918, about the time that Gatsby is fighting in the Argonne. In itself, Jordan's "gay" might mean almost anything, but her next sentence establishes a context: "She had a debut after the Armistice, and in February she was presumably engaged to a man from New Orleans" (p. 50). There can be no real doubt that Daisy's being gay again in chapter 4 and her moving again with the season in chapter 8 refer to the same activity: her full reentry into social life, into its potentiality for romantic commitments, and hence into a jeopardizing of her fidelity to Gatsby.

Both actions are presented as the initial stage of a process that culminates in Daisy's marriage to Tom. As has been discussed, the chapter 8 account traces this process in terms of Daisy's interior experience; Jordan's narrative in chapter 4 presents the same process as observed from the outside. Further, the form of Jordan's statement emphasizes the sense of process. The statement that Daisy was gay again is a brief sentence opening a new paragraph, the debut and the presumed engagement are presented in coordinated main clauses in the following sentence, and the marriage and its attendant circumstances follow immediately and occupy the balance of the paragraph.

It is well to recall that Daisy is gay again in chapter 4 after Jordan's testimony that she had been limiting her dating to military rejects, and that, before meeting Gatsby: "All day long the telephone rang in her house and excited young officers from Camp Taylor demanded the privilege of monopolizing her that night. 'Anyways, for an hour!'" (p. 49). This clearly seems to be what she returns to when she is gay again, gay *as ever*; and it has an exact equivalent in chapter 8 after she begins to move again with the season: "suddenly she was again keeping half a dozen dates a day with half a dozen men" (p. 101). Even the recurrence of the word *again* insists that in each case Daisy returns to being the belle of Louisville, the cynosure of a world of romantic courtship.

Yet the two accounts pin her return to different times. Daisy is gay again in chapter 4 in the fall of 1918 and, it seems, rather early in the fall. Since the three succeeding actions are all located in time—the debut after the Armistice, the presumed engagement in February, the marriage in June—it may be inferred that the first of these stages in the process is earlier than the temporal indicator of the second, and that she is gay again before the Armistice on 11 November 1918. But she begins to move again with the season only after Gatsby's arrival at Oxford, which he himself in chapter 7 says is in 1919 and which we are told here in chapter 8 (as we do not need to be told) is after the Armistice.

The basic disparity between the two accounts was present in

the manuscript, but again Fitzgerald's revision aggravated the matter somewhat. In manuscript, Jordan's account states: "Then after the armistice she was gay again, gay as ever. In February she announced her engagement to a man from New Orleans—and in June she married Tom Buchanan of Chicago" (MS, p. 87). Even here we have her gay again some months before her letters to Gatsby at Oxford make him apprehensive, but, in the typescript version (and the final text), the detail of Daisy's debut was added to strengthen the sense of process and, by appropriating the "after the armistice" to date it, pushed her being gay again further back in time and increased the temporal disparity from the chapter 8 account.

The temporal aspect of that chapter 8 account was not affected by the book's successive revisions, but its narrative technique contributes to its contradicting the chronology of Jordan's testimony. A detailed discussion of the remarkable achievement of the chapter 8 account has already been presented, indicating how the authenticity and narrative momentum generated in the recreation of Gatsby's affairs is carried over into the recreation of Daisy's. Unfortunately, that transference has a temporal dimension, and, thus, after following Gatsby until his arrival at Oxford, some time in early 1919, the narrative engages Daisy's affairs at the same point in time and locates the initiation of the same process in those affairs that Jordan's account in chapter 4 had located about five months earlier. The problem here is much like those encountered in the present time frame with the faulty integration of relocated materials dealing with Gatsby's past.

One might wish to explain away this contradiction by insisting that Daisy's being gay again in the fall of 1918 refers to some activity different from her moving again with the season in the spring of 1919, or even by devising dating ground rules that would allow her to be both active and faithful. (This would also require finding within Daisy's character cogent motives for doing two different things at two different times.) But the evidence for such distinctions does not exist in the text. All of the specifics of the text—except the time references—establish that both accounts are discussing the same thing: Daisy's return to being what she was before she met Gatsby and what, for a time after his departure, she had ceased being. That Fitzgerald intended some subtle difference between the accounts is enormously unlikely on biographical grounds: he himself was tormented for several months in 1919 by Zelda's being "gay again" and "moving with the season," in spite of her ostensible commitment to him.

There seems to be no way, however ingenious, to reconcile the two accounts. Jordan's narrative is so circumstantial, so validated by eyewitness testimony, and so strategically placed in the narrative flow that one cannot question its reliability. Nor can she be thought to be lying, however dishonest Nick finds her. For her motive in providing the account is to win Nick to the plan to reunite the lovers and the Daisy of her narrative is less sympathetic than the Daisy of chapter 8 for being disloyal sooner.

Yet the chapter 8 account must also be accepted as reliable. Nor can the fact that Gatsby is the ultimate source of most of the detail be interpreted to explain the account simply as a presentation of the events as they appeared from Gatsby's distant and prejudiced viewpoint. Such an interpretation would not only ignore the narrative technique and the strategic placement of this material, it would also significantly distort the character of Daisy.

To reconcile the two accounts, one must posit a Daisy who conceals at least three or four months of social activity, including her presumptive engagement, not just from the literal content of her letters to Gatsby, but from their emotional tone as well. He responds, it will be remembered, to their "quality of nervous despair." Such a character would be far more purposeful, skillful, and self-aware than the Daisy of the novel, who always reacts, who never initiates. The end of the chapter 8 account, in fact, insists on a completely passive character, moved by the currents of her world and having virtually no will of her own.

The temporal disparity between the two accounts is one of Fitzgerald's most significant shortcomings in the management of chronology, because it so directly affects the characterization of Daisy. The more charitably viewed girl of chapter 8 does, after all, remain basically loyal until well after the Armistice; thus, for more than a year. Then, confused by Gatsby's continued absence and badly in need of his strength, she is allured by the glamor of her world, is unknowingly and by degrees drawn into it, and yields only when the momentum solidifies itself in the imposing figure of Tom. The girl of Jordan's account in chapter 4 begins with what might well seem the self-deluding compromise of seeing military and romantic ineligibles; breaks with Gatsby sooner, and, on the evidence of her debut and her presumed engagement, more knowingly; briefly and drunkenly recommits herself to him after receiving his last letter; but, considering her poise at the bridal dinner and the wedding, purposefully crushes her feelings, and marries Tom "without so much as a shiver" (p. 51). By the testimony of her own advocate, this Daisy is far more culpable than the essentially will-less girl of chapter 8.

The chapter 8 account, told from Gatsby's vantage point, leaves

Daisy's affairs after her marriage, but Jordan's narrative in chapter 4 continues the events of 1919, and a number of further chronological difficulties ensue. Jordan states that after the wedding, Tom and Daisy "started off on a three months' trip to the South Seas" (p. 51), to which Tom alludes in the Plaza scene by recalling "Kapiolani" and "the Punch Bowl" (p. 88).[37] But she further reports, "I saw them in Santa Barbara when they came back. . . . That was in August" (p. 51). A three-month trip undertaken after a wedding in June (in the middle of June, according to Daisy in the Plaza scene) will, however, not allow them to return until September.

The Buchanans presumably establish themselves in Chicago in the fall of 1919, although the narrative does not specifically say so. There are, however, two inexplicable statements by Nick relating to that residence. In the opening chapter, Nick discusses his acquaintance with the Buchanans and claims, "just after the war I spent two days with them in Chicago" (p. 4). But during the dinner party, Daisy reminds him, "You didn't come to my wedding" (p. 11), to which Nick replies, "I wasn't back from the war," and she agrees, "That's true" (p. 12). The contradiction is obvious: if Nick hadn't come back from the War by June of 1919, he could hardly have visited the Buchanans "just after the war" in Chicago, to which, in any case, they didn't return until September or October of 1919. And in a novel that makes much of Gatsby's being trapped at Oxford until seven or eight months after the Armistice, Nick's returning ten or twelve months after the Armistice cannot be meant to be assumed without comment.

There is also in chapter 8 an account of Gatsby's return to Louisville after his long delayed discharge from the Army. Again, as with the incarnation passage in chapter 6 and Gatsby's long account in chapter 8, although Gatsby is the ostensible source of the information and Nick the ostensible narrator, the passage verges on the authorial, since it deals in details, moods, and emotions that Gatsby could hardly have expressed to Nick. And again, we are presented with discrepancies.

It begins: "He came back from France when Tom and Daisy were still on their wedding trip," and concludes with Gatsby on the train leaving Louisville through 'the spring fields" (p. 102). First, that Gatsby "came back from France" after having spent his last five months at Oxford is, at the most charitable, imprecise. More significantly, since Tom and Daisy did not leave until after their wedding in June, and since Gatsby's five months at Oxford in 1919 must have kept him there at least until the end of May, "the spring fields" makes no sense. Fitzgerald is seeking a momentary effect of poignancy and mild irony, but he achieves it only at the cost of contradicting his chronology.

In this case, the contradiction can be demonstrated as the direct result of careless revision. The manuscript and typescript versions open this section with "once he had to go to Louisville, on business" (MS, p. 225; Gal., 47), and locate the visit merely in the spring of an unspecified year after Gatsby enters the partnership with Wolfsheim. The error is much like those created in the present time frame by Fitzgerald's moving events on the calendar without awareness of the effect on the coherence of the narrative. It is somewhat more affecting for Gatsby to visit Louisville soon after Daisy leaves, but it is chronologically impossible.

We are not told that Gatsby's train takes him directly to New York for his meeting with Wolfsheim, but the assumption would be reasonable. He has traveled to Louisville "on the last of his army pay," and is "penniless" (p. 102) when he leaves. And Wolfsheim, in the last chapter, recalls meeting Gatsby as "a young major just out of the army . . . so hard up he had to keep wearing his uniform because he couldn't buy some regular clothes" (p. 114).

Earlier, Wolfsheim claimed to have known Gatsby for "several years" (p. 47). Given Fitzgerald's elastic use of *several*, this makes good enough sense: the claim is made at the luncheon "late in July" of 1922, and the partnership seems to go back almost exactly three years, to July or August of 1919. Certainly, Nick assumes a relationship of this duration when he wonders whether Gatsby was Wolfsheim's accomplice in fixing the World Series in October of 1919 (p. 114).[38] But Wolfsheim's further claim of having met Gatsby "just after the war" (p. 47) is hardly accurate; their meeting must in fact be eight or nine months after the Armistice. One might think that Wolfsheim is speaking expansively about the flattering "gonnegtion," but the similar discrepancies about when Nick returned suggest that another minor error is the more likely explanation.

The date of the partnership with Wolfsheim also creates a small problem for Gatsby's boast to Nick that "It took me just three years to earn the money" (p. 59) to buy his house.[39] It is very late in July of 1922 when Gatsby speaks, almost exactly three years since the partnership began. But, since he was already giving parties by May, he must have bought the house about four months earlier. Gatsby is significantly understating his achievement in a context in which understatement can only be a narrative lapse. Interestingly, in the manuscript version, Gatsby's claim is "In less than two years I earned it all" (MS, p. 134).

The next incident in Jordan's account in chapter 4 is the basis for the most obvious chronological incoherence in *The Great Gatsby*: "The next April Daisy had her little girl" (p. 51). This is the April after Daisy's wedding, April of 1920. Thus, her daughter, Pammy, is about twenty-six months old when she is mentioned in chapter 1, and almost twenty-nine months old when she appears briefly in chapter 7. Yet Daisy in chapter 1 says, "She's three years old" (p. 7), and the speech of the little girl who appears in chapter 7 is that of a three-year-old, not a two-year-old. Curiously, Fitzgerald's own daughter, Scottie, celebrated her second and third birthdays during the composition of *Gatsby*, so he should have known the difference.

The contradiction is patent and has been noted elsewhere. Bruccoli, for example, mentions it, and deals handily with a possible resolution: "It would be absurd to conclude that Daisy was on the brink of parturition at the time of her wedding. Fitzgerald simply erred."[40] He rather struggled with this detail in composition: at first the manuscript had "Daisy's child was born about six months later"—later than the August in Santa Barbara, thus about eight months after the wedding; but that version was canceled and the elastic "a few months later" (MS, p. 89) written in.

The remaining references in Jordan's account of events prior to the summer of 1922 present nothing more than minor inconsistencies. Immediately after saying, "The next April Daisy had her little girl," Jordan continues: "and they went to France for a year. I saw them one spring in Cannes, and later in Deauville, and then they came back to Chicago to settle down" (p. 51). This concurs rather well with Nick's earlier remarks: "They had spent a year in France for no particular reason, and then drifted unrestfully here and there wherever people played polo and were rich together" (p. 4). Nick moves the Buchanans about somewhat more than Jordan does, and he does not specifically return them to Chicago, but their drifting could be either before or after, or both before and after, their return.

Jordan's "back to Chicago" supports the inference that Tom and Daisy had already lived there for some time, which, by process of elimination, must be late 1919 and early 1920. Also by process of elimination, the year in France must begin in 1920 and extend to the spring of 1921—the only spring they could have been in Cannes to meet Jordan. The form of Jordan's "Daisy had her little girl and they went to France" seems also to imply that they left fairly shortly after Pammy's birth. Thus, Jordan's talk of meeting them "one spring" is a bit surprising in its vagueness; idiomatically, it is "spring of last year" to which she is referring.

Cumulatively, the Buchanans' travels—a year in France, a three-month honeymoon, some months in East Egg, a stay in Santa Barbara, various driftings here and there—are a little difficult to imagine within the calendar limits of their marriage; at the least the majority of their three years together is away from home in Chicago. There is no contradiction here, only the familiar sense of too many events being huddled into too little time. When one correlates this impression with the contradictions about Pammy's age and Nick's visit, it would seem very likely that Fitzgerald himself had virtually no sense of how long the Buchanans were married.[41]

Some deductions can also be made about the various arrivals in the east. Nick, who "came East ... in the spring of twenty-two" (p. 2), is the latest comer. From the invitation to the Buchanans' in early June, early May seems about right for his settling in West Egg, and gives him five or six weeks to observe the parties at Gatsby's, as the opening of chapter 3 appears to require (pp. 25–26), before he is invited in mid-June. We know from this passage and from the recollection by Jordan and the girls in yellow of having met at Gatsby's "about a month ago" (p. 28) that Gatsby was hosting parties as early as May and, thus, must have arrived in April at the latest. And since, again according to Jordan, "Gatsby bought that house so that Daisy would be just across the bay" (p. 52), the Buchanans' arrival predates Gatsby's. March seems the best available choice for their establishing themselves in East Egg, for, during the dinner party, Nick recalls that when he stopped in Chicago on his way east, "a dozen people had sent their love," invents a gallantry about the town being in mourning for Daisy's absence, and suggests Tom might not "stay in the East" (p. 7). All these indicate that in June, the Buchanans' move is still relatively recent. The arrivals are rather crowded together, and one wonders at the exquisite cooperation of the real estate market with Gatsby's dream. Still, they can be accommodated within a consistent chronology.

There are a number of random events before June of 1922 that have little correlation with anything else, and thus cause no real problems. Gatsby's purchase of a house for his father was "two years ago" (p. 115), and hence in 1920; Catherine's unhappy trip to Monte Carlo was "just last year" (p. 22), and hence in 1921. Gatsby's having "read a Chicago paper for years" (p. 53) in hopes of seeing Daisy's name—he later shows her the clippings (p. 62)—is of somewhat shorter duration than it sounds; as of July 1922, it must be something less than three years.

Myrtle's first meeting with Tom, which she relates to Nick in chapter 2 (p. 24), is unlocated in time, but can be accommodated without contradiction. By early June, their affair is notorious, according to Jordan (pp. 10–11); and by early July, to judge from the appointments of the Washington Heights apartment and the relationship with the McKees, it is of some duration. But this would be consistent enough if Tom had gotten busy with the adultery in April or early May; and, since he has previous dalliances to his credit on his wedding trip (p. 51), at the time of Pammy's birth (p. 12), and shortly before leaving Chicago (p. 88), one can rely on his dispatch.

4

Conclusions

Before reviewing the temporal incoherences in *Gatsby* and attempting to evaluate their significance to the novel's achievement, it may be well to respond—though admittedly imperfectly—to two questions that the preceding discussion might seem to evoke.

First, it would seem natural to ask why, if so many incoherences in fact occur, they have gone all but unnoticed. Ultimately, of course, I do not know why, but, after reading fairly widely in *Gatsby* criticism and actively looking for such notices, I have found only the three or four items mentioned at the beginning of this study.[1]

I think it is probable that the brevity, selectivity, and polish of *Gatsby* have invited the presumption that all such structural patterns as chronology must be under complete control. Further, I suspect this presumption has been greatly strengthened by the general critical praise of the book's artistry, and perhaps most especially by the praise of those who have investigated its progressive revisions and found them masterful. The implication that such things as temporal incoherences ought not to occur has perhaps begotten further implication that they do not occur; readers may have been deflected from looking for them, or even, if any were found, from recognizing what they were or whether they had any significance.

In an oddly oblique way, the myth of Fitzgerald himself as the artistic prodigal who wasted his talent, also, I think, lends support to this presumption. By this scenario—which Fitzgerald himself promoted—*Gatsby* was the single unimpeachable expression of his genius; and, thus, the more perfect the achievement, the greater the talent that produced it, and the more poignant the dissipation of that talent. In this vision of romantic tragedy, things like chronological mistakes are not welcome.

It should, however, be added that there well may be some wider awareness of the book's temporal inconsistencies at a level less formalized than published criticism. At the least, I have met a few people who, in their teaching of *Gatsby*, have become aware that its time schemes are not flawless.

This study's presentation of these materials also, perhaps, evokes a more challenging kind of question: how can these chronological incoherences be of any significance when, in spite of them, *Gatsby* is a masterpiece, or a classic, or a great novel, or an artistic success, or some other superlative commendation? If lurking behind such a question is the presumption that, like all masterpieces, *Gatsby* is perfectly or flawlessly rendered, the question is not being posed, but begged. The only response can be to deny the premise: *Gatsby* is not flawless; q.e.d., . . .

Somewhat less categorically, this sort of objection quite clearly implies that great literary achievement cannot allow for the kind and number of inconsistencies demonstrated here: thus, it would seem to disallow the "flawed masterpiece"—a term and a phenomenon that most would consider of fairly frequent occurrence and far from a destructive or dismissive characterization. If *Gatsby* is, in this sense, a "flawed masterpiece," so too are *Huckleberry Finn*, *Moby Dick*, much of Shakespeare, and almost all of Dickens. So too, for most of its literary life, has been Henry James's *The Ambassadors*; its case is probably unique, but it has, I would submit, some analogical relevance to *Gatsby*.

The Ambassadors was completed in mid-1901 and then cut somewhat to accommodate its serial publication in *The North American Review* from January to December 1903. But when, in the same year, the omitted chapter 28 was restored for the first book-length publication, it was inadvertently placed after, not before chapter 29, presumably because chapter 29 is an afternoon scene and chapter 28 a night scene, though intended, of course, to occur on different days. The error went undetected until 1950 and uncorrected until 1957; for over half a century, all texts of *The Ambassadors* appeared with the two relevant chapters transposed.[2]

Yet during that half-century, *The Ambassadors* developed its reputation as one of the greatest achievements of one of the greatest masters of the art; James himself thought it "frankly quite the best, 'all round,' of my productions."[3] It would be foolish to claim that the rather egregious flaw of the reversed chapters had destroyed the accomplishment of *The Ambassadors*, but perhaps even more foolish not to allow that it is a better novel with its chapters in proper order. So, *mutatis mutandis*, let it be with *Gatsby*.

Perhaps the first point to make about these chronological incoherences, which have been plentifully demonstrated, is that they
are chronological incoherences and nothing else. They cannot
be claimed to be merely colloquial imprecisions within a narrative that is itself formally the relatively colloquial testimony of
the character-narrator, Nick. Such colloquial imprecisions do oc-
casionally occur—for example, Nick's recalling his acquaintance
with Gatsby during "the past month" (p. 42), or his recapitu-
latory references to the "three months" of the summer (pp. 97,
103, 117). But this study has maintained a clear distinction between such occurrences on the one hand, and, on the other, incoherences bearing on the verisimilitude of the narrative. When,
in chapter 5, Nick locates the action by referring to an event
"several weeks" (p. 67) before, and Tom and Gatsby agree in locating the same action by referring to a slightly earlier event
"about two weeks ago" (p. 68), we are simply dealing with incoherence. Colloquial looseness cannot be understood to negate
the lexical meaning of *several* and *two*.

Nor can these temporal incoherences be explained away by
arguing that Nick as narrator is not responsible for the mistakes
that he reports other characters to have made. The narrative
method that Fitzgerald has chosen allows for no such distinction.
Nick, as narrator, says coherently that he came east in the spring
of 1922, and incoherently that he visited the Buchanans in Chicago shortly after the War; relying on Gatsby's information, he
says coherently that Gatsby "took" Daisy one October night, and
incoherently that Gatsby visited the spring fields of Louisville
shortly after she left; he reports coherently the agreement of
Jordan and the girls in yellow on having met a month earlier at
Gatsby's, and incoherently his own agreement with Daisy that
he returned from the War too late for her wedding. Regardless of
whether the statements ultimately prove coherent and regardless
of whether they are formally the direct speech of another character, Nick's direct speech, or Nick's narration based on another
character's information or on his own experience, all are presented as having an equal warrant of reliability.

When Fitzgerald wishes to disassociate Nick from something
said, his methods are to have Nick respond verbally, as with
Jordan's accusation of his dishonesty, or to narrate his unspoken
disagreement, as with Tom's final self-justification, or to allow
the ironic inadequacy of the unacceptable statement to stand for
itself, as with Wolfsheim's valediction on friendship. No such

method is applied to any temporal inconsistency in *Gatsby* for the obvious reason that Fitzgerald did not intend any of them to be inaccurate.

The single possibility in the novel of the deliberate use of temporal reference as a function of character is Wolfsheim's claim to have met Gatsby "just after the war" (p. 47)—literally an overstatement. It would, admittedly, be reasonable enough for Wolfsheim to speak expansively about the flattering "gonnegtion," but for this to be an intentional bit of characterization, one must assume that Fitzgerald knew it was overstatement and, thus, that he also knew the literal truth of the matter. The general evidence, however, of how unsure he was of temporal matters makes it far more likely that even here, with an atypical and virtually inconsequential instance, the inexactitude was the author's, not the character's.

There is, in the case of a few of these incoherences, the bare possibility of reconciling them by presuming further, unreported happenings in the narrative. However, in every case, I think, the presumption will be at odds with the implication of the happenings that the narrative does report. Tom's complaint during the lunch in Manhattan that Nick has been out of touch seems to refer to an unbelievable six or seven weeks, but the difficulty can be circumvented by presuming that Nick has seen the Buchanans in the interim and has then decided to avoid them. Such a supposition, however, would make the unreported visit more critical to Nick's relationship with them than the reported visit in the first chapter, and the general implication of this narrative, like any "novel of selected events," is that it is portraying the more critical events and omitting the less critical.

So, too, Nick's remembrance at Gatsby's second party of enjoying his last party "only two weeks before" (p. 70) will not contradict his statement, six days earlier in the time frame, of not having seen Gatsby for "several weeks" (p. 67) if one imagines that he attended a party at which he did not see Gatsby. But the presumption runs counter to the growing intimacy between the two men, and had the event occurred, the reader might legitimately expect Nick to comment on it, perhaps as evidence of Gatsby's total absorption in his reunion with Daisy.

For the reader to make such assumptions and to supply himself with such data is not to respond to Fitzgerald's novel, but to edit or even collaborate with him. Such assumptions—I think it can be fairly claimed—would occur only to the reader who feels obligated to defend Fitzgerald's temporal control of his narrative.

But proper criticism is neither defense nor indictment, it is dealing with the data the artifact presents. Certainly it makes very
little critical sense to invent further narrative detail to redeem
some individual event from chronological incoherence when the
text presents so many irredeemably incoherent events. In the
face of a dozen clear incoherences, it is far more economical to
presume that a thirteenth actually occurs rather than that it is to
be justified by hypothesizing unreported facts for which there is
no evidence of the author's intention.

The occurrence of so many incoherences suggests that Fitzgerald was either insufficiently aware of or insufficiently concerned
with exactly when things happened in his narrative. To some
degree, both are probably true. He must, one imagines, have been
simply unaware of twice contradicting himself within a dozen
lines of text: the Buchanans' three-month honeymoon begins in
June and ends in August (p. 51), and Wilson disappears for three
hours between about 12:10 and 2:30 (p. 107). The oddly unidiomatic references—the *Jazz History*'s performance "last May"
(p. 33), Jordan's meeting at the Buchanans in Cannes "one
spring" (p. 51), the strange opening of chapter 4 "on Sunday
morning" (p. 40)—also seem to suggest inadequate realization of
where events lie in time. But the evidence that Fitzgerald did not
plot the location of his summer events until finishing the first
five chapters in manuscript suggests too little concern for chronology as well. So, too, does the apparent disguising of the misplacement of Myrtle's party; and further, both his deletion from
the original version of the only two specific summer dates, and
at least some of the evasive "few's" and "several's," look like
deliberate wariness based on some recognition of his own uncertainty.

This weakness of chronological sense manifested itself
throughout every stage of Fitzgerald's composition; even the
manuscript isolates Nick on the day of the murder by keeping
the phone, on which Gatsby hopes Daisy will call, open for long
distance from Detroit. But his heavy revision of the text
multiplied the opportunities for error; and new, incoherent references were added—Nick's claim in chapter 6 of not having seen
Gatsby for "several weeks" (p. 67), for instance—or coherent references were revised to incoherence—for example, Nick's remembrance in the same chapter of his last party "two weeks
before" (p. 70) in place of his recalling his first party "two
months ago" (MS, p. 151).

Previous critical investigations have found the drafts of *The*

Great Gatsby to be evidence of a masterly revision, and it would be tendentious not to recognize the many significant ways in which Fitzgerald improved his novel. But even some of the aspects of his rewriting that have been most admired led to inconsistencies. The minuteness of the revision has been presented as an unalloyed virtue, and Eble, Piper, and Long all comment admiringly—and convincingly—on Fitzgerald's polishing his style by replacing even individual words.[4] But the tight focusing on individual details also sometimes led to the failure to coordinate temporally. Thus, he increased the pathos of Gatsby's return to Louisville by relocating it to a time when Gatsby should still be at Oxford.

But a larger and more significant reservation from the usual critical praise must be entered with regard to the single most admired aspect of Fitzgerald's revision—his relocation of events with the narrative. The placement of Myrtle's party as the second chapter has been much praised for its building of suspense before Gatsby's appearance and for its widening our experience of Nick's fictional world, both of which effects are, in fact, achieved. It has been unnoted, however, that the reshuffling of events in the first four chapters also leads not only to the major defect of chronologically misplacing Myrtle's party, but also to a number of further difficulties concerning the romance between Nick and Jordan, his remembrance of the cheating scandal, the progress of his relationship with the Buchanans, and the major pause in the narrative pacing at the close of chapter 3. Similarly, there has been a critical consensus that Fitzgerald with great success relocated in chapter 6 materials dealing with Gatsby's past so as to achieve a gradual resolution of his mystery, and again the reality of the narrative effect must be conceded. But attendant on this relocation was the introduction of chronological error at the beginning of chapter 6, where some of the new material was placed, and at the beginning of chapter 7, from which some of it was taken.

In fact, throughout every stage in revising *Gatsby*, Fitzgerald all but invariably created chronological inconsistency when he relocated events. It might be noted that he moved the Myrtle's party chapter in going from manuscript to typescript, and the materials on Gatsby's past in going from typescript to revised galleys. And it should be emphasized again that none of the praiseworthy narrative effects he achieved by positioning events necessitated the temporal inconsistencies that accompanied them: relocating the Dan Cody story attained a gradual revelation of the truth of Gatsby's past, but connecting it to Tom's visit by a contradictory time reference was merely an error. The evidence seems very clear that, although Fitzgerald's revisions undoubtedly made *Gatsby* a better novel, a more careful and thorough revision would have improved it even further.

That judgment leads very directly to the last and most difficult of this study's concerns—the question of how significant these temporal inconsistencies are, to what degree they limit the achievement of the novel. Needless to say, they are not totally destructive; in spite of them, there is a great deal to admire in *Gatsby*. But they are indeed significant, because time is so heavily emphasized in the novel. Bruccoli reports that there are at least 450 time words in *Gatsby*, and that (excluding character names) *time* itself is the second most frequent noun.[5] The temporal inconsistencies are, however, even more significant because of the ways in which time is utilized both in relation to the symbolic and thematic core of the novel and as a formal element in its narrative structure.

Time in *Gatsby* is, among other things, symbolic of the limitations and imperfections of Gatsby's world, within which there is no significant object to satisfy his yearning for the transcendent. Gatsby's romantic absolutism may perhaps be illuminated by comparing it to the defense that Shakespeare's Troilus makes for retaining Helen from the Greeks—"What's aught but as 'tis valued?" (II, ii, 52). And the existential fact of the world that denies and destroys his insistence on shaping reality in the image of his subjective perception may be shown by the response of Troilus's more pragmatic brother, Hector:

> But value dwells not in particular will.
> It holds his estimate and dignity
> As well wherein 'tis precious of itself
> As in the prizer. 'Tis mad idolatry
> To make the service greater than the god.
>
> (II, ii, 53–57)[6]

Gatsby does indeed assume that value dwells in his particular will, and thus commits the mad idolatry of making his service greater than his god. The novel and its narrator, of course, find a kind of grandeur in the mad idolatry, although obviously they judge Gatsby's divinity, Daisy, to be a woefully inadequate object for the service he dedicates to her.

But the novel also seems to insist that Gatsby's dreadfully bad choice of a lady love has meaning beyond itself. Fairly strongly it claims that no adequate object for Gatsby's longings exists in the social reality he inhabits. In general, the novel's portrayal of its frenetic, acquisitive society supports such an idea, and the claim that the virgin landscape of Long Island did indeed present the Dutch explorer "something commensurate to his capacity for wonder" (p. 21) argues that it is history that has robbed Gatsby of the realization of his vision. Such also is the implication of the reminiscences of Dan Cody's economic buccaneering on a frontier that has disappeared and of the judgment that Gatsby's dream already lay buried in "the darkening fields of the republic" (p. 121).[7]

Yet there are also details that seem to push the symbolic meaning of Gatsby's destruction even further, to suggest that frustration of the imaginative vision is inherent in the nature of man's existence in a finite world. The location of his death at the end of the summer implies that it is in the natural order of things for such dreams to briefly flower and inevitably be destroyed; and when the very closing of the novel describes the boats that image human aspirations as sailing upstream against the current of existential limitation and being "borne back ceaselessly into the past" (p. 121), the subject seems to be not just man in the twenties, but man in the world.[8] That the text ends on this phrase firmly establishes the significance of time to the ultimate implications it intends; the imaginative perception and the will to fulfillment are timeless, but they exist within the permanent finitude of temporal existence. Time symbolizes the inevitable frustration of man's longing for the infinite.

Thus, symbolically, it is completely in keeping that Gatsby, the romantic idealist, be the enemy and ultimately the victim of time. He plans to return to Louisville to marry Daisy, "just as if it were five years ago," and when Nick objects, "You can't repeat the past," he replies, "Why of course you can" (p. 73). He insists that Daisy can obliterate their separation by telling Tom she never loved him, but, at the crucial moment in the Plaza scene, Daisy—a consummate pragmatist in her way—cries out, "Oh, you want too much . . . I love you now—isn't that enough? I can't help what's past. . . . I can't say I never loved Tom. . . . It wouldn't be true" (pp. 88–89). The past can't be helped; it is true and irrevocable and continually participating in the present. And this as much as "Tom's hard malice" (p. 98) breaks Gatsby like glass.

As Roger Lewis says, "For Gatsby and for the novel the past is crucial."[9] In *Gatsby*, what has been participates in what now is, and the hero's past enters the narrative so often and so critically not just to clarify narratively his current motives, but also to establish symbolically that he can never fully be the Jay Gatsby of his own imagining—"his Platonic conception of himself" (p. 65)—nor even the reincarnation of the romantic young lieutenant, disguised by "the invisible cloak of his uniform" (p. 99), because he will always be in some part the North Dakota farmboy and Dan Cody's factotum and Wolfsheim's partner and all the other inescapable realities of his past.

But like any symbol, time as symbol in *Gatsby* demands by definition its proper literal presence in the novel. If we see Tom's breaking Myrtle's nose as symbolic of his brutality or his weeping over the dog biscuits as symbolic of his moral obtuseness, there must be a real nose and real dog biscuits. The narrative must adduce literal automobile accidents to make them symbolize privileged irresponsibility and literal ashheaps to make them symbolize sterile hopelessness. Further, these literal realities must in themselves be sufficiently arresting or vivid or concrete to generate the energy to point beyond themselves to further and symbolic meaning. The particularities of the nosebreaking, the dog biscuits, the accidents, and the ashheaps do in fact generate such energy.

The particularity of time in *Gatsby*, on which so crucial a symbolic weight rests, is its elapsing in the lives of the characters. At various moments in the narrative, the major emphasis may be on the speed or the slowness or even the apparent suspension of time elapsing, but surely the most salient aspect is its elapsing coherently, so that every happening is either before or after or simultaneous with every other happening. The measure of such coherence is chronology, and, although there is of course no necessity that every event be capable of exact dating, there is, strictly speaking, a complete necessity that no event violate coherent chronology. Without chronological coherence, the past is not the past and the present not the present, and, without an irrevocable past continuously conditioning the present, time as symbol in *Gatsby* is undermined. It is exactly this essential literal underpinning of the symbolism that the chronological incoherences erode. Cumulatively, the erosion is, I think, very considerable.

But time is utilized in Gatsby not just as symbol, it is also utilized as a formal element in the narration; and here too the chronological inconsistencies weigh against the novel's achievement. The narrative adduces three significantly distinct times: the present of Nick's narration; the proximate past of the summer of 1922; and the more remote past prior to that summer. Structurally, the proximate past of 1922 is central and dominant: it is the time of the story Nick has to tell, the time of Gatsby's losing both his dream and his life, and the time that contains totally Nick's acquaintance with "the man who gives his name to this book" (p. 1). The fictional values of the other two times are defined by their relationships to this central summer experience. The present of Nick's narration is a vantage point from which to look back on it and evaluate it; the events of the more remote past enter the novel to explain how they inform and condition the summer experience.

Accordingly, the dominance of the summer of 1922 determines the form of the narrative. Indeed, the summer of 1922 becomes the norm of the narrative, and divergences to the time of the telling of the story or to events earlier than the summer are usually quite explicitly marked. When we move to the "now" of the narration with the closing section of chapter 3, we have the explicit reminder of Nick as author-narrator, "reading over what I have written so far" (p. 37); the comparable movement at the opening of the last chapter is specified by the time reference "after two years" (p. 109); and in both cases the verb tense shifts to present—"I see I have given the impression . . . " (p. 37); "I still remember . . . " (p. 109). Adversions to the more remote past are similarly indicated as departures from the central time frame of 1922: Jordan's account in chapter 4 is presented as her verbatim testimony; Gatsby's boyhood self-improvement schedule is literally a reproduced document; and Nick as narrator states that he has taken advantage of a "short halt" in Gatsby's affairs (p. 67) to tell the Dan Cody story. Even divergences from the sequence of the 1922 story are ordinarily indicated: Nick claims that Gatsby told him the Dan Cody story "very much later but I've put it down here" (p. 67), and before tracing Wilson's journey, he says, "Now I want to go back a little" (p. 10).

For it is not just "the history of the summer" that is the central and normative narration, it is the history of that summer in proper temporal sequence. It was, in fact, the apparent violation of this sequence to which Maxwell Perkins objected, after reading the large block of past history in the eighth chapter of the typescript version:

> . . . in giving deliberately Gatsby's biography, when he gives it to the narrator, you do depart from the method of the narrative in some

degree, for otherwise almost everything is told, and beautifully told, in the regular flow of it, in the succession of events, or in accompaniment with them.[10]

Each of nine formal divisions into chapters presents itself "in the regular flow of it," relating summer events later than these of previous chapters and earlier than those of subsequent chapters. (Chapter 2 is in fact out of sequence, but does not seem to be so.) Further, there is the curious narrative device of including a temporal reference in the opening sentence of every chapter, with the significant exception of the chronologically misplaced chapter 2. The implication of the device is, of course, that each unit must be immediately placed in time to orient the materials that will follow, that the reader must always be told how far forward he has come. And, as has been noted, the references to "the history of the summer" (p. 4) really beginning with the Buchanans' dinner, to the postclimactic "last night" (p. 121) when Nick visits Gatsby's empty house, and to the retrospective "three months" of Nick's experience—all characterize the summer of 1922 as not just a unity, but a continuum.

It is against this narrative structuring that so many of the summer events are placed in an unlikely, misleading, and even contradictory manner. Against the grain of this narrative structuring, both the temporal indicators and the quality of the events themselves require the reader to somehow experience Myrtle's party in chapter 2 between Gatsby's party in the earlier part of chapter 3 and the final section of chapter 3 on Nick's working, wandering, and beginning his romance with Jordan. Further, the reader is also required to place in his own understanding the Warwick section that closes chapter 3 later than the cab ride that closes chapter 4. The detail of the narrative demands these locations, and the structure forbids them; this is an artistic failure of a serious order.

But the summer as continuum is not simply an implicit criterion that is sometimes violated by a careless time reference. It is a substratum that essentially conditions the meaning of the narrative, as can be demonstrated by reviewing the novel's single most important human relationship—that of Nick to Gatsby, all of which belongs to the summer of 1922.

The relationship is dynamic: it begins in puzzlement, amusement, and moderate attraction, then, after a number of fluctuations toward negative attitudes like distaste and loss of interest, ends in permanent and total allegiance. The fluctuations have perhaps not always been sufficiently stressed, but they are crucial to our endorsing Nick's final commitment. After a month's casual acquaintance, he is ready to dismiss Gatsby as "simply the proprietor of an elaborate road-house next door" (p. 42); on the evening of the second party, he both empathizes with Daisy's revulsion at its vulgarity and defends Gatsby from Tom's charge of bootlegging; when Gatsby reveals the truth of his attendance at Oxford, Nick wants "to get up and slap him on the back," and he adds most significantly, "I had one of those renewals of complete faith in him that I'd experienced before" (p. 86). That faith undergoes a last test when Nick discovers Gatsby at the "despicable occupation" (p. 96) of lurking outside Daisy's house, but, once he intuitively realizes that it was she who killed Myrtle, his allegiance becomes total. He recognizes that Gatsby is "worth the whole damn bunch put together" (p. 103); after the murder, he finds himself "on Gatsby's side, and alone" (p. 109); and, with touching simplicity, he summarizes both for the grieving Gatz and, I think, for himself, "We were close friends" (p. 112).

The fluctuations that precede this final moral position are critical to our responding to it as Fitzgerald wishes, but fluctuation demands the placement of varying attitudes within the chronological continuum. The matter is somewhat more sensitive since the narrative adduces a quite small number of encounters between the two men. On the day of the ride to Manhattan, Nick says he has spoken to Gatsby "perhaps six times in the past month" (p. 42); and surprisingly they seem to meet no more frequently thereafter—only on the days of the reunion, Tom's visit, the second party, the confrontation, and the murder. Since the relationship is based on so few specified meetings, our understanding of the ebbs and flows of Nick's attitudes about it is lessened or even disturbed by our confusion or ignorance as to whether and for how long Nick is out of touch with Gatsby after the reunion and again after the second party.

Chronological order is somewhat less demanding to the meaning of the events of the past, but even here there are elements structured into the narrative that suggest the significance of an event is conditioned by when it occurred in relation to other events. For example, the increasingly more crucial "truths" about Gatsby's past enter the narrative, in general, in inverse chronological order. We learn of Gatsby's heroism in the War and his partnership with Wolfsheim in chapter 4; later in the same chapter, we learn of his most critical and most frequently recalled role in the past, that of Daisy's lover; in chapter 6, we go back to his time as Cody's protégé; and in the last chapter, we discover his beginnings as the North Dakota farmboy with his self-improvement schedule.

Since the past in *Gatsby* so critically vitiates the present, an incoherent past confuses and undermines our appreciation of moments in the present. For instance, we know that, in the first chapter, Nick is resuming a somewhat less than intimate acquaintance with both Tom and Daisy—"two old friends whom I scarcely knew at all" (p. 4); and the narrative seems to specify some acquaintance with them as man and wife, for "just after the war I spent two days with them in Chicago" (p. 4). But the narrative also specifies that Nick had not returned in time for their wedding in June of 1919, that they spent at least three or four months after their marriage traveling, and that Nick has never met Pammy, who was born in April of 1920. When Nick visited them is impossible to know, yet when he visited them would be significant to his apparent ignorance of and dismay at their deteriorating marriage. The past of Nick's prior experience must affect his resuming acquaintance with the Buchanans, yet we cannot understand the quality of that experience because the narrative supplies nothing but contradiction. The elegant "two old friends whom I scarcely knew at all" lacks the narrative data to support its bemused paradox, and we must accept the fictional wish for the deed.

With regard to the last of the novel's three times, the present of Nick's narration, there is, I think, too little to affect the narrative much either positively or negatively. There is, of course, the contradiction between the first chapter and the last about when the narration takes place, and, formally, the device of Nick as author is both ill chosen and insufficiently developed. But neither weakness seems to have appreciable relevance beyond itself.

Most of the preceding analysis of how the chronological inconsistencies affect the achievement of *The Great Gatsby* has in some way adverted to the question of characterization. It is, I think, here that the achievement is most severely limited.

The final note for *The Last Tycoon* is Fitzgerald's famous pronouncement, "Action is character,"[11] and, unarguably, what a character is is a function of what he does. But it is scarcely less true that what a character does is very frequently critically defined by when he does it, and, in *Gatsby*, this dimension of action, and hence of character, is often overlooked. Nick's recalling the scandal of Jordan's cheating was intended in the earliest manuscript version to occur perhaps ten days after the remembrance first eluded him; it is different if it occurs, as in the final text, some six weeks later. His losing touch with the Buchanans was intended in the earliest manuscript version to last about two weeks; it is different if it lasts, as in the final text, nearly two months. And, most critically in terms of characterization, it makes a great difference whether Daisy's disloyalty to Gatsby begins in the fall of 1918, while he is fighting in France, or in the spring of 1919, while he is trapped at Oxford.

It seems to me crucial to our knowledge of what Daisy is to understand not simply that she is an inadequate object for Gatsby's aspirations because she is culpably weak and shallow, but to understand as precisely as possible how culpably weak and shallow she is. Her ultimate inadequacy is obviously the general intention of the narrative, but this hardly takes us beyond the realm of allegory. Fictional realization demands the dramatization of action, and, in this case, the quality of that action, the degree of its culpable weakness and shallowness, is indexed by time. Without knowing the when of her disloyalty, we cannot properly judge it, and, without judging it, we cannot properly know the character. We understand Daisy the enchantress and even Daisy the ill-used wife well enough, but the two contradictory accounts of her disloyalty are virtually all we ever learn of Daisy herself rather than Daisy as someone else's romantic object.

This takes us close, I submit, to the source of the weakness in what was to Fitzgerald's own mind the least successful of the major characters. Around 20 December 1924, he wrote to Perkins, "I'm sorry Myrtle is better than Daisy," and admitted that the Plaza scene "will never be up to mark—I've worried about it too long and I can't place Daisy's reaction."[12] I very much suspect that the failure in what Fitzgerald would have thought of as his knowledge of Daisy stemmed from his inadequate imagining of her life and character apart from the men she charms. Further, I suspect it is this inadequate imagining that is reflected in the contradiction about the temporal location, and hence, the quality of her disloyalty.

The lack of chronological control also works to the detriment of other characterizations. The incoherent progress of her romance with Nick makes Jordan somewhat less convincing, and the requirement of the time scheme that she keep Gatsby's secret for about five weeks is much out of character for her. Again, Fitzgerald himself on the matter: "Jordan of course was a great idea . . . but she fades out."[13] The same requirement of delay is even more troublesome with Gatsby, who in general acts promptly and resolutely, and whose prompt resolution else-where—in his immediate enlistment of Jordan, for example—is presented as characteristic of who and what he is.

It is, however, upon the characterization of Nick that the novel's imperfect handling of time impinges most severely. Here, however, the difficulties result less from faulty time references than from faulty implications that have some temporal dimension. Nick as a character is especially vulnerable to such faulty implication because he is, so to speak, on stage continuously, and *Gatsby* as a novel is especially vulnerable because of the narrative method Fitzgerald has employed.

He has written, by his own formulation, a "novel of selected incidents," in which very few of those incidents are fully presented—only one or two central "scenes" of each chapter. The full meaning of these central incidents depends on their relationships both to other central incidents and to lesser occurrences which may be only briefly presented or included under narrative generalities or even left totally to the reader's presumption. Thus, the significance of what happens at Gatsby's second party is conditioned by the relatively full depiction of his first party, by the comments in the celebrated guest list about who customarily attended, and even by a large number of casual indications of the notoriety and frenetic gaiety of his parties. Sometimes the conditioning of the meaning is quite subtle: Myrtle's providing Catherine as a companion for Nick in chapter 2 has both a contrast and a parallel in Daisy's arch comments in chapter 1 about pairing him off with Jordan.

It is difficult to imagine any narrative method, not excluding Fielding's or Thackeray's, that does not rely significantly on implication as well as explication of meaning to the reader. But the relative significance is extremely high in *Gatsby* not just because Fitzgerald fully dramatizes so few incidents, but also because he utilizes a limited first-person point of view, because his present action is further limited to so brief a time in his characters' lives, and because thematically and symbolically he insists so strongly that the present meaning is vitiated by the past. All of this results in a narrative method in which the coherence of unstated relationships and implicit connections is crucial to the narrative's success. In the case of Nick's characterization, a number of variously faulty implications seem to posit traits much at odds with Fitzgerald's evident intentions. The fault in every case derives from the temporal dimension within which the implication operates.

Since it takes Nick about six weeks after the remembrance first eludes him to recall the scandal of Jordan's cheating, he seems a bit slow minded and imperceptive. But the implication cannot be intentional, since it is so incoherent with the far more central implications of Nick as a sensitive and insightful judge of other people and as sufficiently intuitive about them to guess that Daisy had driven the death car and that Tom had directed Wilson to Gatsby's. The brief passage on Nick's "short affair" with the girl from Jersey City comparably implies a Nick who is a bit of a philanderer, but this too is incoherent and surely unintended. Fitzgerald quite clearly uses the sexual rapacity of Tom, who continually has liaisons with lower-class women, as an index of his moral irresponsibility. The Nick who judges him can hardly be meant to share such behavior, and, in fact, he portrays himself as so scrupulously "full of interior rules that act as brakes on my desires" that he must extricate himself from "that tangle back home" (p. 39) before allowing the romance with Jordan to proceed further.[14]

It also has been noted that there are a rather large number of narrative facts that, cumulatively, seem to imply that Nick is quite casual about his career in securities. The difficulty, I presume, derives from the fact that of the five major characters, it is only Nick who, in the usual sense of the term, works for a living. But the narrative is in largest part the history of his relationship with these more privileged persons, and thus, narratively it is often necessary that Nick be in their company at times that are ordinarily working hours for the less-privileged. There are enough of these times, and during the rather brief period of the summer, that they imply Nick is cavalier about his job. Such an impression is, of course, by no means Fitzgerald's intention. He portrays Nick as quite scrupulous about fulfilling obligations— Nick is "honest," not "careless"—and he even provides some detail on Nick's buying books on finance and banking and studying during the evenings at the Yale Club. This surely represents his intention, but, if we are to follow Conrad's dictum of believing the tale, not the teller, clearly there are narrative implications that contradict the intention.

As the novel stands, the details about Nick's working hours accumulate to create a general implication just as Gatsby's phone calls and Tom's adulteries do. The difference between the cases is not that it is invalid for the reader to draw implication in the first case, but proper in the other two; it is that the implications generated by Gatsby's and Tom's activities are sufficiently controlled and directed toward a desired effect, while those generated by Nick's activities are not.

In the case of Nick's employment during the summer of 1922, the problem was largely that Fitzgerald had posited so many details that bore an implication contrary to his intention. But with the indications about Nick's life before the summer, the problem is exactly opposite: Fitzgerald has failed to posit sufficient detail to avoid an implication he certainly would have wished to avoid. If his activities during the summer of 1922 suggest that Nick is surprisingly casual about his job, his lack of activity before 1922 suggests that he has been generally idle for twenty-nine years. Most unfortunately for Fitzgerald's intentions, the two impressions cohere to suggest a Nick who is and always has been lacking in industry and ambition. We learn extremely little of what Nick was doing since his graduation from Yale in 1915. To be sure, about a year is accounted for by Nick's military service, but beyond this, there is merely the mild romance with the tennis-playing girl with the perspiration mustache. This tiny bit of activity in a social and even recreational context is all we hear of how Nick has spent about six years between the ages of twenty-three to twenty-nine—the critical years that comprise his young manhood, so his reaction to his thirtieth birthday suggests.

Because the narrative fails to suggest any significant action, the reader is tempted to infer that no such action occurred, that Nick had, in effect, done nothing during this time. And the inference seems substantiated by the Carraway family conference to consider his entry into the bond business, and by his father's agreement to finance him for a year. It sounds as if Fitzgerald intended the reader to share Nick's amusement at his family's deliberation, "as if they were choosing a prep school for me" (p. 3). But he has in fact come close to substantiating the premise Nick laughs at—that he is a twenty-nine-year-old adolescent. The autobiographical basis of the incident lends some corroboration. In the summer of 1911, Fitzgerald's relatives in St. Paul held a comparable family council, which decided to send him to the Newman School in Hackensack, New Jersey; significantly, he was fourteen at the time.[15]

A final problem with implication undermining the characterization of Nick. The one substantial piece of his prior history that we learn is his service in World War I. In the book's opening pages, Nick establishes himself as a combat veteran who participated in the "counter-raid" against the "Teutonic migration" (p. 2), and at the very beginning of his relationship with Gatsby is their common service in France, about which they do a little reminiscing. As I have already discussed, the military units with which they identify themselves seem to require that Nick should at least know Gatsby by reputation, and Gatsby in fact says "Your face is familiar" (p. 3). Curiously, these implications prove to be false leads, but even more curiously, the sense of Nick as a combat veteran has disappeared totally during the time of the ride to Manhattan.

During the ride, Gatsby's account of his heroics appears designed for an uninitiated listener, not for the fellow veteran with whom he had earlier recalled the "wet, gray little villages in France" (p. 3). Even Nick's incredulity is based, not on any experience of the reality of war, but simply on the shabby melodramatics of Gatsby's narration. To Nick, the military exploits are of a piece with Gatsby's tales of collecting rubies and hunting big game: "it was like skimming hastily through a dozen magazines" (pp. 43–44). He simply does not know what to make of Gatsby's "Orderi di Danilo," and lamely allows "the thing had an authentic look" (p. 44). Nick the combat soldier, who should have some knowledge, or at least some preconceptions, about small-unit engagements and foreign decorations, seems to have vanished totally from the book.

To indulge in just a little biographical speculation, it is very inviting to suppose that Fitzgerald's imagining of Nick both as wage earner and as combat veteran is thin because his own experience in these areas was thin. Prior to the publication of *Gatsby*, he had held a nine-to-five job only for a few months in 1919;[16] and to his lasting regret, he spent his entire military career in the United States.

But whether or not it was the limitations of his own experience that weakened his imagining Nick's experience, in point of fact, he did not provide Nick either with a past sufficiently resonant or with a present sufficiently articulated to convince us that Nick has accomplishments and purposes of his own. At various points in the narrative, Nick is an industrious apprentice in the bond business, a scrupulously honorable man in his relations with women, and an experienced soldier. But he is never any of these things firmly or consistently enough. These implications generated by these narrative data simply dissipate, often in the face of contradictory implications generated—surely unintentionally— by other narrative data.

The problem ultimately is time. For by positing a narrative detail with a temporal dimension—such as Nick's age or his military service or his relationship with the girl back home or even his working for a living—the author imposes upon himself not just the necessity of maintaining coherence with other temporal data, but also the necessity of controlling the implications generated by the detail and maintaining their coherence with implications generated by other details. A minimally energetic twenty-nine-year-old must have done something in his recent past; a combat veteran cannot stop being a combat veteran; a man cannot be both casually predatory and painfully scrupulous in his relations with women; an industrious worker must industriously work.

There is a fair amount of *Gatsby* criticism that posits some kind of moral shortcoming in Nick as a constitutive part of Fitzgerald's design. As I have indicated, I do not find such analysis persuasive; it seems to me very clear that Nick was intended to discover and to announce the ethical discriminations the novel has to make. I very much suspect, however, that these incoherences in his characterization have been sometimes perceived as purposeful limitations of his human value. But the shortcomings, I think, are Fitzgerald's, not Nick's.

The total list of shortcomings claimed by this study that bear on the achievement of *Gatsby* and that are rooted somehow in its handling of time is very considerable. It may, in fact, seem as if this study is close to suggesting that they are totally destructive of that achievement. This is of course not my intention; even if all the shortcomings claimed here are allowed, there is still a very great deal that is admirable in *Gatsby*.

But these very real values are, it seems to me, a good deal more located within individual passages and sections of the novel than is usually claimed. This judgment, I think, does Fitzgerald no injustice. He wrote and revised the novel in chapters as if they were more self-contained units than elements of a larger whole. And his penchant for relocating particular details in new and frequently quite different settings sometimes seems more a desire to salvage favorite particularities than to shape the progression of events more artfully. Certainly, the latter interpretation cannot be seriously maintained with regard to Myrtle's party or the "reading over" transition or the cab ride with Jordan when one considers where they were originally placed and where they were relocated.

There is further evidence of Fitzgerald's fondness for salvaging favorite particularities. When one reflects that the "bulbous fingers" (p. 114) of Meyer Wolfsheim were transplanted from Myrtle Wilson (MS, p. 85), it appears that Fitzgerald wanted "bulbous fingers" somewhere in his novel and went looking for a place to attach them; as Long says, "Fitzgerald hoarded his phrases."[17] Even stronger evidence is the fact that there are individual phrases and passages in *Gatsby* that first saw print in the original versions of various short stories collected in *All the Sad Young Men*. For example, as Bruccoli tells us, "the description of Judy's home [in "Winter Dreams"] was lifted from the magazine text of the story and written into *The Great Gatsby* for Daisy Fay's house."[18] And the attitude described here is exactly the one Fitzgerald expressed to Perkins on about 20 December 1924: "But his [Gatsby's] long narrative in Chapter VII will be difficult to split up. Zelda also thought it a little out of key, but it is good writing and I don't think I could bear to sacrifice any of it."[19]

This is, of course, not to claim that *Gatsby* is totally without effective structuring elements. Although there are errors in the detail of Nick's narration and the progression of the summer, both devices shape the narrative with some success. And, to be sure, there are themes and images recurring throughout the novel with unifying force: the use of color has often been noted, and the surprising number of cars and car accidents is arresting and coherent to book's criticism of its society.[20] Even the power of a character conception such as Tom operates as a cohesive force. I would judge, however, that the force of such elements is a good deal more a matter of the sheer imaginative strength, and hence consistency, of their formulation, rather than an indication of careful and calculated structuring.

In his recent biography, LeVot has characterized Fitzgerald as "more poet than novelist," and, in the sense of the imaginative power noted above, this is, I think, quite accurate. But LeVot also speaks of "the stern Jamesian aesthetic" prevailing in the novel and offers as a summary judgment that Fitzgerald was one of the few American writers "to accord primary importance, in the Flaubertian tradition, to problems of structure and the artfulness of writing."[21] To my mind, this is a classic overstatement of how much of the achievement of *Gatsby* rests on Fitzgerald's artistry of construction and his command of traditional fictional categories such as plot and character, rather than the brilliance of its constituent details. That the achievement is very considerable and the details brilliant is not at issue, but claims such as LeVot's for the consummate artistry of design and construction must, I believe, be tempered in view of the chronological incoherences noted in this study.

To be sure, there is a level at which the reader may simply ignore them in reading and responding to *Gatsby*. For sixty years, I expect, many readers have, with relatively little cost, suppressed their awareness of Pammy's two ages. And since most of the temporal incoherences are even less obtrusive—indeed, I have stressed that they have been almost unnoted—it may seem that the data of which this study rests are irrelevant, since they seldom surface above the level of consciousness in reading. But to stipulate that only what registers during a relatively unreflective surface reading is valid for artistic experience or critical evaluation would be a very strange position to take for any work of fiction.

It would be an enormously strange position to take on *Gatsby*, for overwhelmingly, criticism of the novel has asserted that its greatness as fiction resides in its totally successful disposition of particularities to attain artistic ends. The integration of its narrative details has been claimed to be nearly flawless, certainly exquisitely well performed. Fitzgerald's ambition "to write something *new*—something extraordinary and beautiful and simple + intricately patterned:"[22] has been much quoted, and its attainment generally conceded. Victor A. Doyno's summation is quite representative (except perhaps for its reservation): "And a knowledge of the ways in which the novel is 'intricately patterned,' from minor details up to large structural units, partially explains how Fitzgerald created a novel that is 'something extraordinary and beautiful and simple.'"[23]

The intricate patterning of minor details has been asserted to an astonishing degree of particularity. Bruccoli claims a "symbolic identification of Tom with Wolfsheim"[24]—and he may well be right—when Tom goes "into the jewelry store to buy a pearl necklace—or perhaps only a pair of cuff buttons" (p. 120), over seventy pages after Wolfsheim's display of the "finest specimens of human molars" (p. 48). Milton R. Stern claims an especially long list of specifics: "The tapestry of what I have called 'stunning details' is woven into final wholeness of idea not only by threads of cars, names, houses, regions, and time, but also by image-patterns of flowers, colors, lights, sun, heat, moon, and coolness."[25]

For LeVot, Fitzgerald's color symbolism actually seems to bespeak a metaphysic: "Finally, yellow and blue become primary elements, essential qualities toward which gravitate the material and spiritual principles on which the specific character of Fitzgerald's work is based. They can rightly be considered the monads of his imaginary cosmos."[26] And, finally, it may be well to repeat here Long's categorical assertion that temporal details are to be included within the intricate patterning of the novel: "Fitzgerald's handling of time may deservedly be called masterful; time broken up and scattered through the work has been used in every instance with maximum aesthetic effect . . ."[27]

Yet it is hard to see why we should be impressed—as Robert D. Lehan tells us we should[28] —with Fitzgerald's utilization of the clock Gatsby almost knocks off Nick's mantelpiece (p. 57), or the "overwound clock running down" (p. 61) to which Nick likens him, or the clock that ticks on his washstand while "a universe of ineffable gaudiness spun itself out" in his adolescent dreams (p. 65), but pay no attention to what those instruments exist to measure.

The temporal failings in Gatsby are failings in verisimilitude, and it is on this quality of fiction that thematic or symbolic meanings depend for their validity. If Daisy looked like Catherine or if Gatsby's house looked like Nick's, his "following of a grail" would be absurd. To repeat Eble's dictum, "It is, however, only because of the excellence of the particulars that general meanings suggest themselves."[29] If in Gatsby, "five years" or "three months" or "several weeks" or "spring" or "just after the war" or "nine thirty" do not mean consistently and coherently what they should mean, then the particulars are somewhat less than excellent and the general meanings somewhat less than validly established.

There is beyond any argument a great deal to admire and appreciate in Gatsby—elegant language, powerful evocation, great energy, excellent dialogue, fascinating characterizations, marvelously well-rendered scenes. But as for its being a perfectly executed fiction—as Thomas Wolfe once told Fitzgerald—"Flaubert me no Flauberts, Bovary me no Bovarys."[30]

This study began with a series of extravagantly enthusiastic critical claims for The Great Gatsby. Although it argues that the extravagance should be tempered because of the chronological incoherences it has presented, it would not quarrel with the basic enthusiasm. The incoherences are, I believe, a real and significant limitation on the novel's achievement, but I would not wish to overstate the significance of the limitation.

Frederick J. Hoffman's judgment seems to me the correct one:

> Of the great values of The Great Gatsby there can be little doubt. There may be differences concerning the proper weighting of these values or the exact margin of success in any given instance.[31]

One of the margins, I submit, is considerably narrower than had been thought.

Notes

Chapter 1. Introduction

1. James E. Miller, Jr., *F. Scott Fitzgerald: His Art and His Technique* (New York: New York University Press, 1964), p. 139.

2. William A. Fahey, *F. Scott Fitzgerald and the American Dream* (New York: Thomas Y. Crowell, 1973), pp. 64, 72.

3. Maxwell Geismar, *The Last of the Provincials: The American Novel, 1915–1925* (Boston: Houghton Mifflin, 1943), p. 315, n. 3.

4. As cited by William Goldhurst, *F. Scott Fitzgerald and His Contemporaries* (New York: World Publishing, 1963), p. 58; Wilson made the remark in a 1952 memorial to Christian Gauss.

5. Brian Way, *F. Scott Fitzgerald and the Art of Social Fiction* (London: Edward Arnold, 1980), p. 118.

6. Harold Bloom, "Introduction," in his *F. Scott Fitzgerald: Modern Critical Views*, ed. H. Bloom (New York: Chelsea House, 1985), p. 1.

7. Matthew J. Bruccoli, "Introduction," in *New Essays on "The Great Gatsby,"* ed. M. J. Bruccoli (Cambridge: Cambridge University Press, 1985), p. 2.

8. As quoted by George Garrett, "Fire and Freshness: A Matter of Style in 'The Great Gatsby,'" in *New Essays*, p. 103.

9. Ibid., p. 108.

10. Charles Thomas Samuels, "The Greatness of 'Gatsby,'" *Massachusetts Review* 7 (1966):794; reprinted in *Fitzgerald's "The Great Gatsby": The Novel, the Critics, the Background*, ed. Henry Dan Piper (New York: Charles Scribner's Sons, 1970), p. 159.

11. F. Scott Fitzgerald, *The Crack-Up*, ed. Edmund Wilson (New York: New Directions, 1945), p. 9.

12. All noted in Matthew J. Bruccoli, *Apparatus for F. Scott Fitzgerald's "The Great Gatsby" (Under the Red, White, and Blue)* (Columbia: University of South Carolina Press, 1974), pp. 40, 33, 137–38, 43.

13. Citations from *Gatsby* refer to the Scribner Library/Student's Edition (New York: Charles Scribner's Sons, 1957).

14. Miller, *Art and Technique*, p. 114.

15. Kenneth Eble, *F. Scott Fitzgerald*, Twayne's United States Authors Series, 2d ed. (New York: Twayne, 1977), p. 97.

16. Robert E. Long, *The Achieving of "The Great Gatsby": F. Scott Fitzgerald, 1920–1925* (Lewisburg, Pa.: Bucknell University Press, 1979), p. 128.

17. Long, *Achieving*, p. 138, 139.

18. Ibid., p. 140; Long's italics.

19. Bruccoli, *Apparatus*, pp. 118–19, 121.

20. Matthew J. Bruccoli, *Some Sort of Epic Grandeur: The Life of F. Scott Fitzgerald* (New York: Harcourt Brace Jovanovich, 1981), pp. 373, 362.

21. The manuscript is readily accessible in a photographic facsimile: *F. Scott*

Fitzgerald, "The Great Gatsby": A Facsimile of the Manuscript, ed. Matthew J. Bruccoli (Washington: Microcards Editions, 1973); hereafter referred to as *Facsimile.* Bruccoli's excellent introduction is the source of this description and should be consulted for further information on the process of composition of *Gatsby* and the nature of the drafts that survive. References to the manuscript of *Gatsby* (always preceded by MS) are to the page numbers of *Facsimile,* not to Fitzgerald's repetitive numbering within the holograph. Citations from the manuscript have been edited to the extent of omitting cancellations and correcting misspellings.

22. Some bits of these earliest stages survive in the manuscript: the names "Dud" instead of "Nick" (MS, pp. 29, 33), and "Ada" instead of "Daisy" (MS, pp. 58, 92, 93) occur, as Bruccoli notes; and, in one version of the confrontation chapter, Tom appears to be meeting Gatsby for the first time ("Is this Mr. Gatsby?" [MS, p. 165]), as if none of their three earlier encounters had been planned.

23. These are in Bruccoli's own collection. He reports that their provenance is unknown (*Facsimile,* p. xxvii). I have not examined these, but their text is completely legible in the revised galleys to be described below. In imitation of Bruccoli's usage, I will use the word "typescript" to denote this version of the novel. There may be some illogicality in referring to a nonextant document, but it seems a lesser evil than the awkward and probably confusing designation of "unrevised galleys" for the mediate version and "revised galleys" for the final version.

24. I was provided with microfilm of the revised galleys through the courtesy of Princeton University Library.

25. Letter to Perkins, ca. February 18, 1925, in F. Scott Fitzgerald, *Dear Scott/ Dear Max: The Fitzgerald-Perkins Correspondence,* ed. John Kuehl and Jackson R. Bryer (New York: Charles Scribner's Sons, 1971), p. 4 (hereafter referred to *Dear Scott/Dear Max*).

26. Bruccoli (*Facsimile,* p. xxxiv, n. 25) lists these alterations; a couple of them were not made until the second printing in August 1925. The Scribner Library edition, used as a reference text for this study, also embodies revisions based on Fitzgerald's notations in his copy of the first printing; one such revision—Nick's and Gatsby's army units (p. 31)—is of relevance here. For full information on these matters, see Bruccoli, *Apparatus,* pp. 36, 54, 93.

27. Kenneth Eble seems to have published the first significant work on the draft materials with "The Craft of Revision: *The Great Gatsby,*" *American Literature* 26 (1964): 315–26; reprinted in *"Gatsby": Novel, Critics, Background,* pp. 110–17. Eble includes some reference to this work in his later *F. Scott Fitzgerald.* There are also many valuable judgments on the subject in Henry Dan Piper's *F. Scott Fitzgerald: A Critical Portrait* (New York: Holt, Rinehart and Winston, 1965), especially pp. 137–54. The introduction to Bruccoli's *Facsimile* includes not only an excellent explanation of the stages of composition, but also a number of sound analytical and evaluative judgments. The most recent of these studies is Long's *Achieving;* see especially "Appendix: The Manuscript Versions of *The Great Gatsby,*" pp. 185–205.

28. A. Scott Berg, *Max Perkins: Editor of Genius* (New York: Dutton, 1978), p. 68.

29. Letter to Thomas Wolfe, in F. Scott Fitzgerald, *The Letters of F. Scott Fitzgerald,* ed. Andrew Turnbull (New York: Charles Scribner's Sons, 1963), p. 552 (hereafter referred to as *Letters*).

30. *Dear Scott/Dear Max*, p. 89.
31. *Letters*, p. 358.
32. Ibid., pp. 341–42.
33. Bruccoli, *Some Sort of Epic Grandeur*, p. 215; see also *Facsimile*, p. xix, n. 11.

Chapter 2. The Chronology of the Present

1. Samuels, "The Greatness of 'Gatsby,'" p. 784.
2. Garrett, "Fire and Freshness," p. 111.
3. Ibid.
4. Ibid., p. 112.
5. Tom's adultery needs no demonstration; Daisy's—which I think most readers assume anyhow—seems established by Nick's bemusement "that anyone should care in this heat whose flushed lips he kissed, whose head made damp the pajama pocket over his heart!" (p. 76).
6. That Nick lies at Gatsby's inquest, rather as Marlow lies to Kurtz's fiancee in *Heart of Darkness*, is claimed by Gary J. Scrimgeour, "Against *The Great Gatsby*," *Criticism* 7 (1966): 75–86; reprinted in *Twentieth-Century Interpretations of "The Great Gatsby*," ed. Ernest Lockridge (Englewood Cliffs, N.J.: Prentice-Hall, 1968), p. 71. I very much doubt that Fitzgerald consciously implied that this happened, nor do I think that the published text makes it necessary for the reader to assume that it did.
7. Scrimgeour, Ibid., has presented a somewhat analogous judgment of this matter. He contrasts, to Fitzgerald's disadvantage, his device of Nick as author to Conrad's presentation in *Heart of Darkness* of Marlow as a character telling his tale to his companions on the yacht. For Scrimgeour, Fitzgerald fails totally to include in *Gatsby* any sense that the story has an existence apart from Nick's telling it and, thus, "that the narrator may be giving us a truth that is anything but unvarnished;" and further, "that it is exactly here ... that Fitzgerald's artistic and ethical inferiority lie" (p. 72).
8. Bruccoli, *Apparatus*, pp. 118–19.
9. Garrett ("Fire and Freshness," p. 113) speculates that the newspapers may be implied as Nick's source.
10. Later Nick does in fact tell Jordan, "This Mr. Gatsby you spoke of is my neighbor—" (p. 10), and she remembers it at the party (p. 28).
11. Both manuscript (MS, p. 74) and final text (p. 15) call Eckleburg "a wild wag of an oculist," but an oculist is an M.D. who specializes in the treatment of the eyes and who until very recently did not advertise. As the spectacles on the billboard make clear, Eckleburg is actually a wild wag of an optometrist.
12. Frederick J. Hoffman "Introduction," in his *"The Great Gatsby": A Study* (New York: Charles Scribner's Sons, 1962), p. 9.
13. Piper, however, does state: "As far as plot is concerned, Chapter II is an unnecessary digression" (*Critical Portrait*, p. 139).
14. If one wishes to locate the party on the 1922 calendar, Saturday, 17 June, is much the best choice, although the twenty-fourth is not completely impossible. Dealing this closely in days, however, creates the awkwardness of beginning the tournament on a weekday, since if Gatsby's house is dark, it is presumably not a Friday when Daisy speaks of Jordan's playing "to-morrow" (p. 13).

15. The Bronx-Whitestone Bridge across Long Island Sound did not open until 1939.

16. According to Fitzgerald's letter to Perkins, ca. 20 December 1924 (*Dear Scott/Dear Max*, p. 90), Jordan was based on Edith Cummings, who had been a school friend of Fitzgerald's first love, Ginevra King, and who had won the Women's Championship at the Rye-Biltmore Country Club in 1923, the summer that the Fitzgeralds lived in Great Neck.

17. According to the logic of pronoun reference, Fitzgerald has had Nick say that "the events of three nights" absorbed him less than his personal affairs "much later." Thus, he has clearly implied that at some later time, the events of those nights absorbed him more. The intention, of course, is that between antecedent and pronoun, the events of three nights transpose themselves by a species of synecdoche into "Gatsby's affairs," which is the meaning we take from the text, although not quite what it says. Comparably, Fitzgerald has English idiom somewhat wrong with "three nights several weeks apart." This does not mean "three nights, the third of which is several weeks later than the first"; it means "three nights, the last two of which are several weeks later than the first and second respectively." Compare the usage in "three children several years apart" or "three revolutions several decades apart" or "three disasters several centuries apart."

18. Dan P. Seiters, *Image Patterns in the Novels of F. Scott Fitzgerald*, Studies in Modern Literature, No. 53 (Ann Arbor, Mich.: UMI Research Press, 1986), p. 71.

19. Eble, *F. Scott Fitzgerald*, pp. 90–91.

20. *Facsimile*, p. xxiv.

21. There are actually two versions of the guest list in manuscript: the earlier in composition has the date "July 5th, 1923" (MS, p. 260); the latter "July 5th, 1921" (MS, p. 63). The changes in the year will be discussed in the section on the novel's past chronology.

22. Bruccoli, however, is surely right in claiming that "such horology fosters the impression of historical time" (*New Essays*, p. 12).

23. In spite of my frequent adverse judgments on Fitzgerald's revisions, I must in fairness pay this compliment: Tom's dialogue here is the only passage in either manuscript or typescript that seems to me regretably omitted; and even here, Fitzgerald's decision (I presume) that it was too long for the scene was probably right.

24. The situation is only a little less troublesome in the manuscript version in which Jordan does not say that she suggested a luncheon in New York "immediately" and therefore at the beginning of the conversation, but only as Nick walks into the library to end it (MS, p. 92). Still, the sense that Gatsby had selected Nick before learning that he is Daisy's cousin is implicit in the episode from its origin. It might also be noted that Jordan further reports that Gatsby was unaware that Nick is "a particular friend of Tom's" (p. 52), and one must assume it easier to discover that both men are Yale '15 than that a Carraway from somewhere in the northern midwest is the "second cousin once removed" (p. 4) of a Fay from Louisville.

25. Thomas A. Hanzo evidently reads the incident similarly, for he calls the cab ride "a scene in which Jordan easily accepts Nick's first attentions"; see his "The Theme and Narrator of *The Great Gatsby*," *Modern Fiction Studies* 2 (1956–57):189; reprinted in *Twentieth-Century Interpretations*.

26. Fitzgerald often used cab rides as the setting for romantic dalliance.

James R. Mellow, in his *Invented Lives: F. Scott and Zelda Fitzgerald* (Boston: Houghton Mifflin, 1984), drawing on the unpublished autobiography of the lady involved, traces the kiss in the victoria back to the initiation of "an odd, rampantly sexual episode" in August 1919 between Fitzgerald and Rosalinde Fuller. Mellow notes comparable uses of cab rides in "Myra Meets His Family," "The Lees of Happiness," and *Tender Is the Night*; strangely, however, he calls the victoria ride in *Gatsby* "a chillingly cruel scene," and mistakenly (but instructively for the point at issue here) says that during it, Nick "convinces himself, briefly, that he is in love" (p. 84).

27. See the table on p. 61.

28. Revision of Galley 26; reprinted in *Facsimile*, p. 271.

29. The dating in the manuscript of the reunion on 3 July may be thought to argue against the two-day interval between it and the luncheon, which in the manuscript occurs in "June" (MS, p. 65) and, therefore, seemingly, at least three days earlier. But the manuscript chronology is often imprecise, and like the final text, the manuscript contains the implication in the opening conversation that the reunion will be "the day after tomorrow" (MS, p. 125).

30. *Letters*, p. 341.

31. *Dear Scott/Dear Max*, pp. 76, 80; Fitzgerald's emphasis.

32. 20 April 1925, *Dear Scott/Dear Max*, pp. 100–1.

33. Mencken's review appeared in the Baltimore *Evening Sun* (2 May 1925), p. 9; reprinted in *Gatsby: Novel, Critics, Background*, p. 121. Fitzgerald's response is in his letter to Edmund Wilson, Spring 1925; reprinted in his *The Crack-Up*, p. 270.

34. F. Scott Fitzgerald, *The Great Gatsby* (New York: Modern Library, 1934), p. viii.

35. On 18 June 1924, Fitzgerald wrote Perkins that he was considering adding another 16,000 words to *Gatsby*, which, he claimed, would bring it almost to the length of *This Side of Paradise* (*Dear Scott/Dear Max*, p. 72). At the time he should have been well into the manuscript version, and—if one can trust his arithmetic—thinking of a novel of perhaps 65,000 words or more.

36. If one accepts the dating of the party on Sunday, 2 July, Nick is making a four-day weekend of it.

37. In the manuscript, as Nick arrives at work, Gatsby's chauffeur checks the dashboard clock and comments, "'Bout three quarters of an hour" (MS, p. 78), apparently the time of the trip, including a stop for gas.

39. The reporter's visit, incidentally, is the only summer event in the last four chapters that is relocated in the sense that many events of the earlier chapters are. Literally, the visit "about this time" could possibly precede the reunion. But clearly Fitzgerald thought of it as later, as I expect all readers do.

39. Perkins had actually said something a little different: "in giving deliberately Gatsby's biography, when he gives it to the narrator, you do depart from the method of the narrative in some degree" (*Dear Scott/Dear Max*, p. 84). The elements of first-person narration by Gatsby in the typescript version Perkins had read may account for his judgment, but he did also advise that some of Gatsby's biography "come out, bit by bit, in the course of the actual narrative."

40. To be more precise, it is *at least* "several weeks" since Gatsby's reunion with Daisy, to allow for the possibility of some unreported meeting with Nick after the reunion. As will be seen, however, "several weeks" since the reunion is in itself a contradiction, and increasing the period would be superfluous to examining the chronological incoherence.

41. Again, in the interests of precision, the lunch with Wolfsheim is *at least* two days before the reunion, since, as has been explained, it is just possible that it be a little more than two days earlier. Again, however, assuming an earlier point of reference would only aggravate the contradiction, which can be sufficiently demonstrated without further supposition.

42. If there is an inequality, the "*only* two weeks" between Nick's parties (AE) is less than the "*about* two weeks" between the lunch and the visit (BD).

43. This change occurred in an early draft of the revision of Galley 30; Fitzgerald coded it "A. Galley 30." A number of such drafts were preserved with the manuscript, although they are, of course, significantly later in time of composition. The passage in question is reproduced in *Facsimile*, p. 274.

44. Nick says, "She made my bed and cooked breakfast" (p. 2), and she has left for the day when, "at eleven o'clock" (p. 55) on the morning of the reunion, Nick remembers that he needs her.

45. "For a week after . . ." appears in the hand-written draft of galley revision "A. Galley 34," with everything but "For a week" subsequently crossed out; the draft is reproduced in *Facsimile*, p. 282. In "A. Galley 34" itself—the type-written slip that Fitzgerald pasted to Galley 34—the typed copy reads, "For a week I didn't see him and I became gradually more aware . . . ," but all of this is crossed out in pen and "Only gradually did I become aware . . ."—the reading of the final text—written in above.

46. That as close a reader as Seiters simply asserts, "The lights fail to go on next Saturday" (*Image Patterns*, p. 70), perhaps suggests that this is the more natural inference.

47. The confrontation scene is also located on a Saturday later in the manuscript version: Wilson keeps his garage open because "there was lots of business on Saturday night" (MS, p. 202, Seq. E). This, too, was cut before the typescript version, where, as in the final text, the confrontation must occur on a weekday because Nick hears the noon whistles as he returns from work to lunch with the Buchanans. Oddly, the detail of the whistles first appeared in Sequence A (MS, p. 164), implicitly contradicting the Saturday reference four pages earlier in the same sequence.

48. The "half holiday" here and Tom's "Look at that line of cars headed for the country" (MS, p. 88, Seq. D) suggest that Fitzgerald may at one time have intended to locate the action during the Labor Day weekend. If so, nothing survived even into the typescript version.

49. Alternative Sequence B omits the incarnation passage, but retains somewhat different versions of Gatsby's lamentation and his song, although we are spared most of the lyrics (MS, pp.175–77).

50. The latter date does in fact result in a temporal incoherence; see below, p. 89.

51. Strictly speaking, the final version would allow the reporter's visit to be either in the very last days of July or the very first of August. But since it appears in a chapter otherwise totally devoted to August events, very probably it always in Fitzgerald's mind belonged to the later month.

52. All of the relevant details appear as early as the manuscript: Wilson's phone call (MS, p. 165); his claim to have gotten "wised up" two days before (MS, p. 173); his finding the leash "yesterday afternoon" (MS, p. 230); even the three o'clock reference (MS, p. 229). The contradiction is not quite absolute: one could devise a two-day growth of Wilson's suspicions culminating in his discovery of the dogleash about 12:15 P.M. on Monday—technically, in the

afternoon—followed by a dash to get Tom on the phone by 12:30. But that Fitzgerald intended any such thing is simply not to be believed.

53. *Dear Scott/Dear Max*, p. 99.

54. This is from Sequence D. The earlier, and rejected, Sequence C puts the confrontation at a cafe, not the Plaza, but its time references are in substantial agreement: it is "late afternoon" (MS, p. 183) when the group leaves the Polo Grounds for the cafe, "half past seven" when the confrontation ends, and "almost eight" (MS, p. 187) when they leave for Long Island.

55. Reprinted in *Facsimile*, p. 308.

56. Seiters, in his discussion of communication images in *Gatsby*, states that "the telephone, in fact, breaks off communication" (*Image Patterns*, p. 61); although he provides a number of convincing instances, curiously, he neglects this one.

57. It may be noted that the detail is actually a corroboration of the fact that Myrtle's party in chapter 2 is out of chronological sequence. On the same night, Nick reflects on the Buchanans' dinner "three months before" (p. 97), and on the next morning on Gatsby's first party, also "three months before" (p. 103). But Myrtle's party, which separates them, is only "a couple of months ago."

58. The process of softening the detail begin in typescript with the dropping of the word "all" before "bruised" and the substitution of "this" for "the words bruised and broken" (Gal., 50).

59. Although the geography is very different in the manuscript, the time references were present from the earliest version (MS, p. 234).

60. Bruccoli insists on this several times; see his *Apparatus*, pp. 117–18, 119–20, 122, and 128–30.

61. The typescript (Gal., 51) changes this to the reading of the final text.

62. Neither Wolfsheim, a Jew, nor Stella, "a lovely Jewess" (p. 113), should be working on the Sabbath, although admittedly neither seems especially devout.

63. Andre LeVot, in *F. Scott Fitzgerald: A Biography*, trans. William Byron (Garden City, N.Y.: Doubleday, 1983), locates the Plaza scene in September and claims "Gatsby is murdered a few days later and is buried in a downpour six days after his defeat" (p. 118). Of these temporal locations, first is all but surely wrong, the second categorically wrong, and the last without basis in the text.

64. Slagle's call was added in galley revision (A. Gal., 52), and is thus another, though minor, instance of Fitzgerald's revising temporal incoherence into the text.

Chapter 3. The Chronology of the Past

1. In the manuscript there are five summer references, confined to two places in the text: two—one a cancellation of the other—occur during Jordan's meeting the lovers in Louisville (MS, pp. 85, 86); the other three—two are cancels—link their dancing at the second party to an earlier summer night (MS, pp. 149, 150). The three-year references occur during the reunion, when Gatsby says it is "three years and two months" (MS, p. 130) since he has seen Daisy, and during the conversation after Gatsby's second party, when Nick says to him, "You wait three years and then after three weeks you're tired" (MS, p. 161, canceled). The earliest version of the guest list in chapter 4 is on a timetable "in effect July 5th, 1923" (MS, p. 260), later revised to "July 5th, 1921" (MS, p. 63); the manuscript also has Nick coming east "in the spring of

twenty-one" (MS, p. 4). In the typescript version, the 1921 date for the timetable (Gal., 19) and the remembrance of the lovers dancing on an earlier summer night (Gal., 31) survive. At the reunion, Daisy says that she and Gatsby haven't met "in over three years," but his immediate reply is "five years next February" (Gal., 27). This exchange makes it clear that these survivals in the typescript are no more than inadvertances. Gatsby's "February" correlates with the manuscript version of Jordan's narrative, in which Daisy actually does go to New York to see Gatsby off to the War (MS, p. 92).

2. These were jotted on the endpaper of his copy of Malraux's *Man's Hope* (1938). Bruccoli's *Facsimile* reproduces the notes and identifies most of the references; see pp. xvi–xvii.

3. The stories are "Diamond Dick and the First Law of Woman" and "Rags Martin-Jones and the Pr_nce of W_les," as noted by Long, *Achieving*, p. 208, n. 23.

4. The manuscript contains six five-year references: MS, pp. 17 (a cancel), 87, 91, 149 (two cancels), and 158.

5. *Dear Scott/Dear Max*, pp. 83, 89. In the typescript version Perkins read, Nick says, "He was only a little older than me" (Gal., 15). The older man whom Fitzgerald had in mind was probably Edward M. Fuller, of the Fuller-McGee financial scandals, to whom he refers later in the same letter. Both Piper (*Critical Portrait*, p. 115) and Long (*Achieving*, p. 79) call Fuller a "thirty-nine year old bachelor," apparently his age around the time of his four criminal trials in 1922 and 1923.

6. In manuscript, Cody's affair with Ella Kaye occurs in "1903" (MS, p. 218), and she defrauds Gatsby "in the spring of nineteen thirteen" (MS, p. 220). The latter detail, but not the former, survived in the typescript version. The revision to the final copy seems intended to make Gatsby just a bit older.

7. The anomaly here presumably is responsible for so careful a reader as Eble calling Gatsby "an obscure second lieutenant" (*F. Scott Fitzgerald*, p. 90) when he meets Daisy. Fitzgerald changed the commission from second to first lieutenant during galley revision (Gal., 21).

8. As Bruccoli notes (*Apparatus*, p. 127). Something of the same judgment seems implied in Perkins' advice to let the truth of Gatsby's military service come out gradually in the narrative (*Dear Scott/Dear Max*, p. 84).

9. Gatsby's two-week attendance at St. Olaf College (p. 65) belongs somewhere in this time, but causes no problem. It can be accommodated easily even if one insists (as seems unnecessary) that it occur at the beginning of a spring or fall semester.

10. Wheeler Winston Dixon, in his *The Cinematic Vision of F. Scott Fitzgerald*, Studies in Modern Literature, no. 59 (Ann Arbor, Mich.: UMI Research Press, 1986), claims that "Fitzgerald provides Nick with an extensive biographical background, giving his narrator a depth which aids in fleshing out Nick as a character" (p. 27). He may be relying on the references to Nick's father and more generally on those to the ambience of being a Carraway in Nick's home town; but Dixon presents no instance of Nick's adult activity that is not considered here.

11. The study most noted in this regard is R. W. Stallman's "Gatsby and the Hole in Time," *Modern Fiction Studies* 1 (1955):2–16. Keath Fraser's "Another Reading of *The Great Gatsby*," *English Studies in Canada* 3 (1979), reprinted in Bloom's *Modern Critical Interpretations*, pp. 57–70, might also be noted: Fraser finds Nick unreliable in that he continually conceals his own sexual

ambiguity, including his attraction to Mr. McKee. Both Hanzo's ("Theme and Narrator") and Scrimgeour's ("Against *The Great Gatsby*") articles survey the various critical opinions about Nick's moral reliability.

12. The matter is neatly posited both by Scrimgeour: "If the reader cannot accept Carraway's statement at face value, then the integrity of the novel is called in question ("Against *The Great Gatsby*," p. 77); and by Hoffman: ". . . if we cannot accept Carraway, the novel is a chaos" ("Introduction," p. 14).

13. One might wish to argue that Fitzgerald intended "twenty-one" to indicate full maturity rather than an exact age. Such a resolution is unconvincing, however; for, in manuscript and typescript, Tom is only "twenty" (MS, p. 8; Gal., 2) at the time of his greatest fame. The revision was clearly an unsuccessful attempt at chronological accuracy.

14. Zelda Sayre was born on 24 July 1900, and was not quite eighteen when she met Fitzgerald.

15. In manuscript, Myrtle is "approaching middle age" (MS, p. 99).

16. Robert Sklar, *F. Scott Fitzgerald: The Last Laöcoon* (New York: Oxford University Press, 1967), p. 183.

17. Miller, *Art and Technique*, p. 117.

18. Ibid., p. 109; Sergio Perosa, *The Art of F. Scott Fitzgerald*, trans. Charles Martz and Sergio Perosa (Ann Arbor: University of Michigan Press, 1965), p. 74.

19. Sklar, *Last Laöcoon*, p. 192.

20. Lionel Trilling, *The Liberal Imagination* (New York: Viking Press, 1950), p. 253.

21. As will be discussed later, p. 136, virtually all of this detail first appeared in the magazine version of "Winter Dreams."

22. Miller, *Art and Technique*, pp. 108–9.

23. Garret, "Fire and Freshness," p. 113.

24. Miller, *Art and Technique*, p. 111; the quote is from Fitzgerald's *The Last Tycoon*, ed. Edmund Wilson (New York: Charles Scribner's Sons, 1941), pp. 139–40.

25. Garrett, "Fire and Freshness," p. 112.

26. Ibid., pp. 112–13, 114.

27. "Gatsby and the Failure of the Omniscent 'I,'" *Denver Quarterly* 12 (1977), reprinted in Bloom's *Modern Critical Interpretations*, pp. 47, 55.

28. Ibid., p. 50.

29. Ibid., pp. 53, 54, 55.

30. There is evidence in the drafts (MS, p. 92; Gal., 27) that Fitzgerald once planned to have Daisy go to New York, probably in February, to see Gatsby off. See above, pp. 145–46, n. 1.

31. In F. Scott Fitzgerald, *Three Novels of F. Scott Fitzgerald*, ed. Malcolm Cowley (New York: Charles Scribner's Sons, 1953); see also Bruccoli, *Apparatus*, pp. 36, 54, 62, 93.

32. Bruccoli, *Apparatus*, pp. 39, 55, 63, 95.

33. Ibid., pp. 39, 36.

34. Ibid., p. 127. Bruccoli further notes that the First Division—Gatsby's division in the text of the first edition—did serve in the Argonne Forest.

35. The northern edge of the Argonne Forest was cleared about two weeks before the Armistice, but the plural in "after the Argonne battles" makes it most unlikely that Fitzgerald had such a distinction in mind.

36. The typescript version differs verbally, but not substantially: "I was only there a few months. . . . A lot of the officers had a chance to go there after the

war" (Gal., 45). Note that the time of Gatsby's stay went from "six months" to "a few months" to "five months"—further indication of Fitzgerald's use of "few" (like "several") to evade more precise indications of time. See above, p. 000.

37. These are tourist spots in Hawaii, as identified by Bruccoli, *Apparatus*, pp. 134, 35.

38. There is also a manuscript version that puts Gatsby's meeting with Wolfsheim in "that flushed, feverish spring" of 1919 (MS, p. 246).

39. Another minor discrepancy: Nick speaks of the two mansions flanking his bungalow as "huge places that *rented* for twelve or fifteen thousand a season" (p. 3; italics added); as noted by Bruccoli, *Apparatus*, p. 33.

40. Bruccoli, *Apparatus*, p. 121. Actually, when Daisy married in June, she would have been two months over the brink of parturition. Bruccoli simply erred.

41. The confusions on this matter, one presumes, account for Perosa's mistaken reference to Daisy's "four years with Tom" (*The Art of F. Scott Fitzgerald*, p. 68).

Chapter 4. Conclusions

1. See above, pp. 12–13.

2. See Henry James, *The Ambassadors*, Norton Critical Edition, ed. S. P. Rosebaum (New York: Norton, 1964); cf. especially Rosebaum's "Editions and Revisions," pp. 353–67.

3. Quoted by Rosebaum, in Ibid., p. 358.

4. Eble, *F. Scott Fitzgerald*, pp. 92–93; Piper, *Critical Portrait*, p. 154; Long, *Achieving*, pp. 200–2.

5. Bruccoli, *New Essays*, p. 11; Bruccoli's ultimate source is Andrew T. Crossland's *Concordance to "The Great Gatsby"* (Detroit: Gale Research, 1975). Appropriately, only *house* (95 times), which so often suggests status or accomplishment, is more frequent than *time*, which so often adverts to the impending destruction of those values.

6. Quotations are from *The Riverside Shakespeare*, ed. G. Blakemore Evans (Boston: Houghton Mifflin, 1974), p. 461.

7. Marius Bewley has perhaps written most insightfully on Gatsby's story as symbolically related to the myth of the American Dream. He speaks of Gatsby's "sentimentality," but locates it in "the difficulty of expressing, in the phrases and symbols provided by his decadent society, the reality that lies at the heart of his aspiration." See his "Scott Fitzgerald and the Collapse of the American Dream," in his *The Eccentric Design* (New York: Columbia University Press, 1957); reprinted in *F. Scott Fitzgerald: Modern Critical Views*, p. 45.

8. So Seiters reads the final image as showing "man's helplessness in an accidental universe. . . . This accurately describes man's plight" (*Image Patterns*, p. 83).

9. Roger Lewis, "Money, Love, and Aspiration in *The Great Gatsby*," in *New Essays*, p. 47. Bruccoli (*New Essays*, p. 11) has a consonant interpretation of the incident from which this study takes its title. When Gatsby almost knocks the broken clock off Nick's mantle, and then "set it back in place" (p. 105), Bruccoli comments, "The irony of this symbolism may be too blatant. Gatsby, the time defier, rescues a defunct timepiece, but time will put him 'back in place.'"

10. *Dear Scott/Dear Max*, p. 84.

11. Fitzgerald, *The Last Tycoon*, p. 163.

12. *Dear Scott/Dear Max*, p. 89.

13. Ibid.

14. If one takes the word "affair" to denote a sexual relationship, the contradiction is even stronger. But I presume that what Fitzgerald had in mind here would have derived rather immediately from his own sexual attitudes at the time, and what these might have been has been so muddied by Hemingway's one-upmanship in *A Moveable Feast* that even an intelligent guess seems impossible.

15. Bruccoli, *Some Kind of Epic Grandeur*, p. 32.

16. He worked at the Barron Collier Advertising Agency in New York City from February to May 1919 and, amazingly, for a couple of weeks in September 1919 as a common laborer for the Northern Pacific Railroad; see Ibid., pp. 96, 102.

17. Long, *Achieving*, p. 32.

18. Bruccoli, *Some Sort of Epic Grandeur*, p. 174. The original version is conveniently available in his *New Essays*, p. 10.

19. *Letters*, p. 170.

20. The most extensive discussion of this topic in *Gatsby* is Seiters, *Image Patterns*, pp. 57–87.

21. LeVot, *Biography*, pp. 166–67, 98–99, ix.

22. Letter to Perkins, ca. July 1922. F. Scott Fitzgerald, *The Correspondence of F. Scott Fitzgerald*, ed. Matthew J. Bruccoli and Margaret M. Duggan, with Susan Walker (New York: Random House, 1980), p. 112.

23. Victor A. Doyno, "Patterns in *The Great Gatsby*," *Modern Fiction Studies* 12 (1966–67), 426; reprinted in *"Gatsby": Novel, Critics, Background*, p. 167.

24. Bruccoli, *Facsimile*, p. xxviii.

25. Milton R. Stern, *The Golden Moment: The Novels of F. Scott Fitzgerald* (Urbana: University of Illinois Press, 1970), p. 262.

26. LeVot, *Biography*, p. 152.

27. Long, *Achieving*, p. 140; his italics.

28. Robert D. Lehan, *F. Scott Fitzgerald and His Craft of Fiction* (Carbondale: Southern Illinois University Press, 1966), pp. 118–19.

29. Eble, *F. Scott Fitzgerald*, p. 97.

30. Letter of 26 July 1937, quoted in Fitzgerald, *The Crack-Up*, p. 325.

31. Hoffman, *"The Great Gatsby": A Study*, p. 17.

Bibliography

Berg, A. Scott. *Max Perkins: Editor of Genius.* New York: Dutton, 1978.

Bloom, Harold, ed. *F. Scott Fitzgerald: Modern Critical Views.* New York: Chelsea House, 1985.

Bruccoli, Matthew J. *Apparatus for F. Scott Fitzgerald's "The Great Gatsby" (Under the Red, White, and Blue).* Columbia: University of South Carolina, 1974.

————. *Some Sort of Epic Grandeur: The Life of F. Scott Fitzgerald.* New York: Harcourt Brace Jovanovich, 1981.

————, ed. *F. Scott Fitzgerald, "The Great Gatsby": A Facsimile of the Manuscript.* Washington: Microcards Editions, 1973.

————, ed. *New Essays on "The Great Gatsby."* Cambridge: Cambridge University Press, 1985.

Crossland, Andrew T. *Concordance to "The Great Gatsby."* Detroit: Gale Research, 1975.

Dixon, Wheeler Winston. *The Cinematic Vision of F. Scott Fitzgerald.* Studies in Modern Literature, No. 59. Ann Arbor, Mich.: UMI Research Press, 1986.

Eble, Kenneth. *F. Scott Fitzgerald.* Twayne's United States Authors Series, 2d ed. New York: Twayne, 1977.

Evans, G. Blakemore, ed. *The Riverside Shakespeare.* Boston: Houghton Mifflin, 1974.

Fahey, William A. *F. Scott Fitzgerald and the American Dream.* New York: Thomas Y. Crowell, 1973.

Fitzgerald, F. Scott. *The Correspondence of F. Scott Fitzgerald.* Edited by Matthew J. Bruccoli and Margaret Duggan, with Susan Walker. New York: Random House, 1980.

————. *The Crack-Up.* Edited by Edmund Wilson. New York: New Directions, 1945.

————, and Maxwell Perkins. *Dear Scott/Dear Max: The Fitzgerald-Perkins Correspondence.* Edited by John Kuehl and Jackson R. Bryer. New York: Charles Scribner's Sons, 1971.

————. *The Great Gatsby.* New York: Modern Library, 1934.

————. *The Great Gatsby.* Scribner Library/Student's Edition. New York: Charles Scribner's Sons, 1957.

————. *The Last Tycoon.* Edited by Edmund Wilson. New York: Charles Scribner's Sons, 1941.

————. *The Letters of F. Scott Fitzgerald.* Edited by Andrew Turnbull. New York: Charles Scribner's Sons, 1963.

————. *Three Novels of F. Scott Fitzgerald.* Edited by Malcolm Cowley. New York: Charles Scribner's Sons, 1953.

Geismar, Maxwell. *The Last of the Provincials: The American Novel, 1915–1925*. Boston: Houghton Mifflin, 1943.

Goldhurst, William. *F. Scott Fitzgerald and His Contemporaries*. New York: World Publishing, 1963.

Hoffman, Frederick J. *"The Great Gatsby": A Study*. New York: Charles Scribner's Sons, 1962.

Lehan, Robert D. *F. Scott Fitzgerald and His Craft of Fiction*. Carbondale: Southern Illinois University Press, 1966.

LeVot, Andre. *F. Scott Fitzgerald: A Biography*. Translated by William Byron. Garden City, N.Y., 1983.

Lockridge, Ernest, ed. *Twentieth-Century Interpretations of "The Great Gatsby."* Englewood Cliffs, N.J.: Prentice-Hall, 1968.

Long, Robert E. *The Achieving of "The Great Gatsby": F. Scott Fitzgerald, 1920–1925*. Lewisburg, Pa.: Bucknell University Press, 1979.

Mellow, James R. *Invented Lives: F. Scott and Zelda Fitzgerald*. Boston: Houghton Mifflin, 1984.

Miller, James E., Jr. *F. Scott Fitzgerald: His Art and His Technique*. New York: New York University Press, 1964.

Perosa, Sergio. *The Art of F. Scott Fitzgerald*. Translated by Charles Martz and Sergio Perosa. Ann Arbor: University of Micigan Press, 1965.

Piper, Henry Dan. *F. Scott Fitzgerald: A Critical Portrait*. New York: Holt, Rinehart & Winston, 1965.

———, ed. *Fitzgerald's "The Great Gatsby": The Novel, the Critics, the Background*. New York: Charles Scribner's Sons, 1970.

Rosebaum, S. P., ed. *The Ambassadors*, by Henry James. Norton Critical Edition. New York: W. W. Norton, 1964.

Seiters, Dan P. *Image Patterns in the Novels of F. Scott Fitzgerald*. Studies in Modern Literature, No. 53. Ann Arbor, Mich.: UMI Research Press, 1986.

Sklar, Robert. *F. Scott Fitzgerald: The Last Laöcoon*. New York: Oxford University Press, 1967.

Stallman, R. W. "Gatsby and the Hole in Time." *Modern Fiction Studies* 1 (1955): 2–16.

Stern, Milton R. *The Golden Moment: The Novels of F. Scott Fitzgerald*. Urbana: University of Illinois Press, 1970.

Trilling, Lionel. *The Liberal Imagination*. New York: Viking Press, 1950.

Way, Brian. *F. Scott Fitzgerald and the Art of Social Fiction*. London, Edward Arnold, 1980.

Index